35180
Angelina Grimke: Voice of
Abolition
Ellen H. Todras
AR B.L.: 9.3
Points: 8.0

# ANGELINA GRIMKÉ

Angelina Emily Grimké Weld

# ANGELINA GRIMKÉ
## VOICE OF ABOLITION

by

ELLEN H. TODRAS

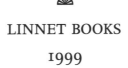

LINNET BOOKS

1999

First published 1999 as a Linnet Book,
an imprint of The Shoe String Press, Inc.,
North Haven, Connecticut 06473.

Library of Congress Cataloging-in-Publication Data

Todras, Ellen H., 1947–
      Angelina Grimké : voice of abolition / by Ellen H. Todras.
            p.      cm.
      Includes bibliographical references (p.      ) and index.
      ISBN 0-208-02485-9 (lib. cloth : alk. paper)
      1. Grimké, Angelina Emily, 1805–1879—Juvenile Literature.
2. Women Abolitionists—United States—Biography—Juvenile
literature. 3. Abolitionists—United States—Biography—Juvenile
literature. 4. Antislavery movements—United States—History—19th
century—Juvenile literature. 6. Women's rights—United States—
History—19th century—Juvenile literature. I. Title.
      E449.G865T63      1999                          98–42931
      973.7′114′092—dc21                              AC
      (B)

The paper in this publication meets the minimum requirements of
American National Standard for Information Sciences—Permanence of
Paper for Printed Library Materials, ANSI Z39.48–1984. ∞

Designed by Sanna Stanley
Printed in the United States of America

*To Mark—*
*who always believed*

*And to Syd Skolsky—*
*who taught me about the first step*

# CONTENTS

# ACKNOWLEDGMENTS

I owe thanks to many people for aiding in the completion of this book: to the staff of the Clements Library, University of Michigan, where the Weld-Grimké Papers are housed; to the South Carolina Historical Society, for use of its collection; to Charleston Public Library and Charleston Visitor Center for helpful information; to the staff of the Historical Society of Pennsylvania and the Free Library of Philadelphia; and to Nancy Hannan of Hyde Park Historical Society in Boston. At both the Eugene Public Library and the Knight Library, University of Oregon, the research librarians were always helpful.

Much gratitude goes to previous biographers of Angelina and Sarah Grimké, and of Theodore Weld: Catherine Birney, Katherine DuPre Lumpkin, Larry Ceplair, Benjamin P. Thomas, Robert H. Abzug, and especially Gerda Lerner.

Thanks to Professors Tom Hager, Barbara Welke, and Martha Ravits of the University of Oregon for their advice and encouragement; thanks to Gerda Lerner, Professor Emeritus of the University of Wisconsin, for the sharing of information; thanks to Joan LeVine for information on Eagleswood and enthusiasm for the project; and thanks to Rhoda Jenkins and Coline Jenkins-Sahlin for providing a photograph of Elizabeth Cady Stanton. All illustrations are credited in captions except for the engravings of Angelina and Sarah Grimké, and Theodore Weld used in sidebars; also William Lloyd Garrison. These are from *William Lloyd Garrison: The Story of His Life, Told by His Children*.

The members of my writers' group—Carol Shelton, Beverly Reicher, Deb Rice, and Barb Stevens-Newcomb—unfailingly gave sound advice and support. Thanks to my young reader, Sarah Hurwit.

Thanks to editor Christine Michaud for making me examine the odds and ends I first ignored; and thanks to publisher Diantha Thorpe for her belief in this project.

Finally, I could not have completed this book without the constant support of my husband Mark and my children, Ben and Ani.

# Author's Note

Over the past century and more, common American spelling and usage have changed somewhat. For the most part, I have tried to maintain the phrasing and spelling of those who are quoted in this book, with several exceptions.

The word *antislavery* was hyphenated in the 1800s (*anti-slavery*) but is a compound word now. I have kept the hyphenated spelling when quoting someone in the past, or in the names of antislavery societies of that time; I have used the modern form otherwise. The phrase "woman's rights"—today "women's rights"—is correct for the time. I have been unable to find when the singular became the plural.

Quotations in the text are from letters and diaries, or have been reprinted from books as noted in the bibliography. Also, Angelina Grimké often used dashes in her letters to separate her sentences; in most cases, I have changed these dashes to periods to make her writing easier to read.

# ❧ I ❧

# BRAVING
# THE MOB

O N MAY 14, 1838, abolitionists and other reformers in
America were thrilled by the opening of beautiful
Pennsylvania Hall in Philadelphia. This huge hall had been
erected as a haven for free speech, because the antislavery
cause was so controversial that speakers could not find halls
to rent for their lectures. To build Pennsylvania Hall, 2,000
people—many of them women—had bought $20-shares as
part-owners.

But the very day after the hall opened, notices were posted
throughout the city calling for a mob to gather outside the hall
the following night. An excerpt from those posters read:

> A convention to effect the immediate emancipation of
> the slaves throughout the country is in session in this
> city, and it is the duty of citizens who entertain a
> proper respect for the Constitution of the Union and the
> right of property to interfere, *forcibly*, if they must.

For these citizens, freedom for slaves threatened both private
property rights (for slaves were property) and the sanctity of
the Constitution (for slavery had been accommodated in that
document). They were particularly incensed by blacks and
whites meeting together, sure that such communion would lead
to "amalgamation," mixing of the races.

Convention organizers, worried by the threat of violence in these posters, asked the mayor of Philadelphia to provide them with police protection—indeed, with good reason, since just three years earlier a race riot had gripped the city for days. Mayor John Swift refused the reformers' request, however, expressing amazement at their lack of confidence in the good sense of Philadelphians.

EVENING, MAY 16, 1838. A hostile, noisy crowd surrounded Pennsylvania Hall. The mob hurled jeers and insults at the 3,000 abolitionists, mostly women, who entered the hall that evening for a meeting of the Anti-Slavery Convention of American Women. These reformers were aware that abolitionist gatherings had provoked violence before. They must have wondered, that night, whether violence against them would be the price of free speech.

Inside, free blacks and whites sat shoulder to shoulder as William Lloyd Garrison, publisher of the abolitionist newspaper *The Liberator*, gave the opening address. When he finished, the mob hissed him and then shoved into the hall, "yelling and shouting," Garrison later recalled, "as if the very fiends of [hell] had suddenly broke loose." In an effort to maintain order, the next speaker, Maria Chapman, a leader of the Boston Female Anti-Slavery Society, rose to address the audience. As she began, the mob withdrew from the building, but continued to shout and stamp their feet outside throughout her brief speech—so loudly that she could not make herself heard above the din.

At this point the next speaker strode forward and held up her hand. The audience, which had been stirring uneasily, quieted. Angelina Grimké Weld, the most famous abolitionist speaker of her time, began to address her fellow abolitionists. A bride of just two days, she was tall and graceful, with great, blazing blue eyes and dark curly hair. A Quaker, she wore a plain dress with no frills and a simple, close-fitting bonnet. Yet her simplicity of dress only served to accentuate her strength of character. Angelina's powerful, impassioned voice rang through the hall, exposing the evils of slavery: "I have seen it! I have seen it! I know it has horrors that can never be described. I was brought up under its wing. I witnessed for many years its demoralizing influence and its destructiveness to human happiness. I have never seen a happy slave."*

Bricks and stones crashed through the windows. Shattering glass sprayed the aisles, the audience, and the stage. Her eyes glowing and her slender back straight, Angelina raised her voice and went on.

As a daughter of the South, Angelina was in a unique position to comment on the horrors of slavery. She had grown up in a wealthy South Carolina household with many slaves to wait on the family. She hated slavery and tried to persuade her family to free their slaves. Instead, long, bitter arguments eventually convinced Angelina that her family would not change, and she left home and moved north to Philadelphia when she was twenty-four.

Nine years later, on that May night in 1838, Angelina spoke to the crowd for over an hour, skillfully using the violence of the mob as the counterpoint to her subject. When the crowd outside screamed threats, Angelina retorted, "What is a mob? What would the breaking of every window be? Any evidence that we are wrong or that slavery is a good and wholesome institution?" When Angelina sat down, the applause of the audience was so thunderous that it drowned out the clamor of the mob.

---

*The full text of this speech is in the appendix.

Two other women spoke briefly following Angelina. This was the first time Abby Kelley spoke in public; she was to devote her life to speaking out against slavery. The final speaker, Lucretia Mott, had founded the Philadelphia Female Anti-Slavery Society in 1833. The mob continued its intrusions throughout their speeches. Then, as the meeting adjourned, the audience and speakers left the building as quickly as they could, shouldering their way through the taunting throng outside.

AFTERNOON, MAY 17, 1838. Once again the women of the anti-slavery movement gathered in Pennsylvania Hall, risking their reputations, their safety, their very lives to promote freedom for blacks in America. Some of the mob had stayed through the night outside the hall and continued to threaten reformers who entered. Although hall managers again requested help from Mayor Swift, he claimed he didn't have the police force to protect them. As the day wore on, the crowd grew larger and more unruly. Finally, in an attempt to prevent a riot, the mayor cancelled all evening activities at Pennsylvania Hall.

As women prepared to leave the afternoon session of the convention, Angelina Grimké Weld was anxious for the safety of the black women in the building—for, if there were violence, they would bear the brunt of it. She asked that the white women protect their colored sisters by taking each one of them by the arm while going out. Thus the column of reformers left the building, black and white together. Angelina and the other women must have shamed the rowdy crowd outside, for they grudgingly formed an aisle through which the women safely passed. In the same way that Angelina Grimké Weld confronted slavery and other wrongs, she braved the mob, and at least for that moment, prevented it from causing harm.

Newly built Pennsylvania Hall housed stores and offices for reform societies on its first floor, and auditoriums and a gallery on the second story. It also had a library and committee rooms for meetings. The hall boasted such innovations as gas lighting and a ventilation system. From Webb, *History of Pennsylvania Hall*

It was supposed that Southerners had instigated the riot that led to the burning of Pennsylvania Hall, but nothing was ever proved. An inquiry found the mayor of Philadelphia negligent in his duty to protect the peace. *Courtesy of The Historical Society of Pennsylvania*

NIGHT, MAY 17, 1838. In accordance with the mayor's orders, no groups convened at Pennsylvania Hall in the City of Brotherly Love. Mayor Swift told the mob that they had achieved their purpose in stopping the meeting. He advised them to go home, and then he withdrew. But the mob whooped at the mayor's departure and took the opportunity to ransack the building and then burn it to the ground. By midnight, Pennsylvania Hall was a great smoking ruin. Riots against black people in Philadelphia shook the city throughout the week.

A Philadelphia merchant, Sidney George Fisher, commented on the riot in his diary:

> To be sure there was great provocation. The cause itself is unpopular and justly so. . . . Such is the hatred to abolition here, that many respectable persons, tho they do not defend these outrages, blame them faintly and excuse them.

Many newspapers of the time, including the *New York Commercial Advertiser*, the *Boston Morning Post*, and the *Boston Centinel and Gazette*, echoed the belief that the abolitionists had brought this catastrophe on themselves.

Angelina Grimké was the first Southern woman to speak out against slavery. In the decades before the Civil War, condemning slavery was a perilous business, even in the North. Ugly mobs frequently attacked antislavery speakers; in 1835 William Lloyd Garrison was almost lynched in the streets of Boston. Antislavery printer Elijah Lovejoy was shot and killed in Illinois in 1837 as he tried to defend himself and his printing press from a mob.

Both Northerners and Southerners, slaveholders and abolitionists alike, were astonished when a Southern lady began speaking out against slavery. Not only did Angelina Grimké expose herself to the possibility of physical attack; she also laid herself bare to the certainty of ridicule and verbal abuse from the public at large. For in the 1830s *no woman—certainly no respectable woman—spoke in public.*

At a time when many people in the North were unaware of the horrors of slavery in the plantation South, Southerners like Angelina described the abuses that they had witnessed, even in the best and most gracious of families. Angelina Grimké's mighty speaking presence convinced thousands of Northerners to take up the abolitionist banner. She was among the first American women to speak in public.* She was the first woman in America to address a state legislature. And then, because a respectable woman *was* speaking in public, Angelina forced people to examine their attitudes toward women, and toward women's capabilities. She inspired many future leaders in the suffrage movement, including Elizabeth Cady Stanton and Lucy Stone. The woman's rights movement was born at the lecterns where Angelina spoke out against slavery.

---

*In 1828–1829, Frances Wright, an English woman, lectured in several American cities. She was treated as a freak for these endeavors. Between 1831 and 1833 a black woman, Mrs. Maria W. Stewart, spoke to other blacks in Boston about religion, abolition of slavery, and opportunities for girls. Ultimately, she admitted failure, saying, "I have made myself contemptible in the eyes of many."

# ❧2❧

# TWO KINDS OF
# EDUCATION

Nothing at Angelina Emily Grimké's birth on February 20, 1805, indicated the path her life would take. The fourteenth and final child of wealthy parents of high social standing, Angelina grew up free of economic worries, and with an impeccable pedigree. Her father, John Faucheraud Grimké, had served as a colonel in the Revolutionary War, was a judge of the Supreme Court of South Carolina, and owned a number of successful plantations. His father, of German descent, had been a wealthy merchant in Charleston. Judge Grimké's ancestors on his mother's side were Huguenots, French Protestants who sought refuge in America during the religious conflicts of the 1600s.

Judge Grimké was highly respected among his peers for his great intelligence, honesty, and work ethic. A devout Episcopalian, the judge believed that a combination of piety, discipline, and attention to duty would lead to happiness and usefulness to oneself, one's family, and one's country. He took an intense interest in the raising of his children, although with his many duties he was often absent from home.

Thus the lion's share of raising this large family was left to his wife, Mary Smith Grimké. Polly, as she was nicknamed, was a beautiful, elegant woman. She was a direct descendant of

The stylishness of Angelina's parents as Charleston aristocrats is evident in this set of pictures. This miniature of Mary (Polly) Smith Grimké at the age of twenty-seven gives a hint of the fashionable world her daughters were born to, in sharp contrast to the difficult lives they would pursue. Pierre Henri, watercolor on ivory. *Courtesy of Gibbes Museum of Art/Carolina Art Association*

Judge John Faucheraud Grimké, right, was one of a handful of Southerners at that time with a college degree. A graduate of Cambridge University, England, he published a compilation of South Carolina laws in 1790 which for many years was invaluable to lawyers and judges in that state. *Courtesy of The Historical Society of Pennsylvania*

Thomas Smith, one of the original eight proprietors of Carolina. Polly counted colonial governors among her ancestors, as well as the famed Colonel William Rhett, who delivered Charleston from pirates in 1718. Her father, one of the richest men in South Carolina, was known as "Banker Smith of Broad Street." Polly's elder brother, Angelina's uncle, served as governor of North Carolina and as an aide to George Washington during the Revolutionary War.

Angelina's parents loved each other deeply. Although Polly did not share the judge's intellectual interests, she liked to read

# CHILDREN OF JUDGE JOHN AND POLLY GRIMKÉ

| NAME | BIRTH DATE | OCCUPATION | DATE OF DEATH |
|------|-----------|------------|------|
| John | 1785 | doctor; married | 1864 |
| Thomas Smith | 1786 | lawyer; married | 1834 |
| Benjamin* | 1788 | | 1794 |
| Mary | 1789 | managed family household; unmarried | 1865 |
| Frederick | 1791 | lawyer; unmarried | 1862 |
| Sarah Moore | 1792 | reformer, teacher; unmarried | 1873 |
| Anne* | 1794 | | 1794 |
| Anna | 1795 | teacher; widowed | 1882 |
| Elizabeth Caroline (nicknamed Eliza) | 1797 | managed family household; unmarried | 1874 |
| Benjamin Secundus | 1798 | occupation unknown; unmarried | 1825 |
| Henry | 1801 | lawyer, planter; married | 1852 |
| Charles Faucheraud | 1802 | occupation unknown; unmarried | 1857 |
| Louisa* | 1803 | | 1803 |
| Angelina Emily | 1805 | speaker, teacher; married | 1879 |

*died in infancy or childhood*

religious tracts. Her life centered on household matters and children. She enjoyed the gay social life of Charleston, and family accounts are sprinkled with references to numerous visits to and from the homes of friends and relatives. In the twenty years between 1785 and 1805, Polly bore fourteen children, three of whom died in infancy or childhood. It was not unusual for people to have large families at this time, nor for children to die in infancy; indeed, the fact that only three Grimké children died before reaching maturity is probably a testament to the good health and medical care that their upper-class family had access to.

Yet the responsibilities of such a large household were taxing to Polly's capabilities, for she had difficulty controlling both her children and her slaves. With her children she was impatient and unyielding; they did not respect her and felt alienated from her. With her slaves, whom she called "my people," she occasionally resorted to severe punishments, such as beatings or whippings.

The great families of South Carolina were limited in number, and, as they intermarried over time, it seemed as if everyone was related to nearly everyone else. Most of the South Carolina aristocracy, to which the Grimkés belonged, lived in the "lowcountry," the tidal plain fronting the Atlantic Ocean. Here well-to-do families established plantations, great farms with hundreds and often thousands of acres; they grew cotton, rice, or indigo along one of the many rivers that emptied into the Atlantic.

These families grew accustomed to a luxurious and gracious lifestyle. Plantation homes were beautiful, spacious dwellings, akin to mansions or even palaces. Rooms were large, ceilings high, and furnishings rich. Foods of all kinds were abundant on the plantations' massive tables. Magnificent gardens adorned the landscape. Boats arriving at the plantation docks delivered fine fabrics and other costly imports from Europe.

This lavish lifestyle had a price: It was built on the backs of slaves. By the time Angelina was born, slavery had existed in the United States for nearly 200 years. Few slaves were left in the North by the 1820s, but the economic well-being of the South and its great plantations was grounded in slavery. Plantations could only be successful with a great quantity of cheap labor, and what could be cheaper than slaves? By 1775, of the approximately 100,000 people living in South Carolina's lowcountry, only 25,000 were white.

Of course, the lives of the slaves were as dissimilar from those of the planters as hell is from heaven. The landowners' great material luxury contrasted with slaves' meager food and clothing. Slaves had no control over any aspect of their existence. Slaveowners, not the slaves themselves, benefited from their labor; owners could even rent out slaves and reap the profit. Marriage among slaves was an informal affair, requiring the permission of owners, but with no legal sanction. Husbands and wives often had different masters and could not live together. In spite of this, a slave's greatest fear was to be sold away from his or her family for the monetary benefit of the owner.

Slaves were denied the advantage of education; in most Southern states it was against the law to teach slaves to read and write. Even their religious activities were regulated and closely supervised.

Slaves had to carry written passes when traveling without a white person. City laws passed in Charleston, South Carolina, in 1806 provide an idea of the restrictions facing blacks at that time: Slaves and free "people of color" could not gather in groups larger than seven except in the case of a funeral or when supervised by a white person. They couldn't dance without permission, make excessive noise, smoke in the streets, or carry a stick unless sickness required it, for a stick might be used as a weapon.

While slavery produced untold suffering among the slaves, it was a primary cause of the wealth of the planter families. Wealth by itself, however, cannot guarantee a happy or productive life. Growing up in a master/slave society had a potentially harmful effect on even the white children's moral and character development. Parents wanted their children to work hard when they grew up, so that the family fortune would increase. But it is difficult to convey the value of work when servants are satisfying every whim. The children of most of the landowning families were dependent on their parents for their inheritance. Usually, upon the father's death, daughters would receive a monetary sum, and the property (plantations, houses, other real estate) was divided among the sons. As young men, waiting to inherit this property, these sons often lacked motivation, and turned to such idle and dangerous pursuits as gambling and drinking. Parents often expressed concern that their sons were developing habits that could ruin their futures.

The older Grimké sons, John, Thomas, and Frederick, chose the respected professions of law and medicine. Judge Grimké worried more about his younger sons, two of whom showed tendencies toward a dissolute lifestyle. Unlike most plantations of the time, the Grimké plantation, Belmont, was located in the Union District in the "upcountry" of South Carolina. It was unusual for a landholder of Judge Grimké's stature to establish a plantation hundreds of miles from the social life of the lowcountry. Having a plantation so far away may have given the Grimké parents more control over the upbringing of their children.

Like many other Southern plantation owners, Judge Grimké initially cultivated rice on his plantations. With the invention of the cotton gin in 1793 and the rise in the price of cotton in the 1800s, however, he turned more and more to growing cotton. Cotton is a highly work-intensive crop, and presumably as Judge Grimké turned more acreage to cotton cultivation, he acquired more and more slaves.

The Grimkés lived on Belmont in the cooler months between November and May. Their mansion at Belmont was located 3 miles from the cotton fields. Years later, Angelina wrote that she really did not know what the slaves' condition on the plantation was like. Although the family wealth was derived from the work of slaves, *Angelina never saw the working plantation.* Close in distance, life at the family home and at the plantation proper were worlds apart. Judge Grimké used overseers to manage his plantation, and very likely his family knew few details of the slaves' lives there. "But this I do know," Angelina later maintained, "that the overseers who had charge of [the slaves], were generally unprincipled and intemperate men."

During the warmer months of the year, the heat and humidity of inland South Carolina were oppressive and conducive to illness. Then the Grimké family moved to their second home, in the beautiful coastal city of Charleston, where ocean breezes brought relief from the heat. Many landowners had homes there, and Charleston offered a gay social season. Horse racing, fox hunts, and cock fights, balls, dances, and concerts all claimed the attentions of the pleasure-loving Charlestonians.

The Grimkés' town house on fashionable Front Street (now called East Bay Street) was a massive four-story structure of over 10,000 square feet. A long, elegant double stairway led up to the front door. Such stairways were common, making it possible for men and women to use separate entrances so that women's ankles were never visible to the opposite sex. The kitchen and storage rooms were on the first floor of the Grimké town house; the judge's offices on the second floor; and the drawing room, a formal room where guests were received and entertained, and bedrooms claimed the upper stories.

Luxurious furnishings adorned the spacious rooms. Judge Grimké's library of books was so extensive that shelves lined the walls of many rooms in the house, indicating the priority of education. Like other Southern families of their social standing, the Grimkés had a large number of household slaves. Housekeepers, parlormaids, seamstresses, laundresses, personal servants, cooks, butlers, and footmen lived in a separate building behind the family home. Angelina's firsthand knowledge of slavery stemmed from this household environment.

When Angelina was born, one of her older sisters, twelve-year-old Sarah, begged her parents to let her be the baby's godmother. Sarah had been devastated by the recent departure of her favorite brother, Thomas, to Yale College in Connecticut. At first her parents refused, but finally they consented, thinking it would give the older girl a sense of purpose. Years later Sarah recalled her reaction after the baptismal ceremony:

> I prayed that God would make me worthy of the task I had assumed, and help me to guide and direct my precious child. Oh, how good I resolved to be, how careful in all my conduct, that my life might be blessed to her!

Sarah and Angelina were devoted to each other, Angelina following Sarah wherever she went. While most people grow apart from their families when they mature, Angelina and Sarah would remain extremely close throughout their lives.

Sarah was a gentle, highly intelligent girl. Born twelve years before Angelina, she had experienced a somewhat different childhood. Then, Judge Grimké was able to spend more time with his children, and Sarah benefited greatly from this influence. Unlike Angelina, Sarah had visited the plantation as a child, and the judge insisted she learn some of the duties of the slaves.

From an early age Sarah loved learning and eagerly joined Thomas in his studies. When he began to learn Latin, however, the judge and Polly would not hear of Sarah participating. "You are a girl," her parents said. "What do you want of Latin and Greek and philosophy? You can never use them." No amount of argument could convince her parents to bend to her wishes, and Sarah's formal learning ceased. Still, Judge Grimké is said to have claimed with pride that if Sarah had been born a boy, she would have made the best jurist in the United States.

Even as a young girl, Sarah was disturbed by the gross inequities of slavery. Against the rules of her household and the laws of South Carolina, little Sarah taught her waiting-maid, Hetty, to read at night behind closed doors, until the pair were discovered and severely reprimanded. While Sarah no longer actively disobeyed the dictums of her society, she continued to sympathize with the slaves and their plight.

Unlike plain Sarah, Angelina was a beautiful child, with dark curls and striking blue eyes. The baby of the family, she was coddled and petted, growing into an outgoing and strong-willed child. Polly Grimké, busy with the cares and responsibilities of managing the large household, often left the raising of Angelina to Sarah. Indeed, Angelina called kindly Sarah "Mother," indicating the role Sarah had in her upbringing. Sarah, a great intellect, encouraged Angelina to think for herself.

Angelina's education was typical of daughters of wealthy Charleston families. Reading and writing were necessities, as

# Sarah Moore Grimké

*Sarah M. Grimké*

At various times in their lives, Sarah and Angelina Grimké served as catalysts to each other's reforming zeal. Certainly it was Sarah who first stimulated Angelina to consider slavery an abomination. Eventually Angelina followed the pattern set by Sarah—leaving home, moving to the North, and becoming a Quaker.

After that, Sarah joined the more self-reliant Angelina in the life of an antislavery activist. Sarah contributed several notable works to both antislavery literature and the budding woman's rights movement. Her *Epistle to the Clergy of the Southern States* (1836) demanded of Southern clergymen how they could reconcile slavery and Christianity. In her *Letters on the Equality of the Sexes and the Condition of Woman* (1838), Sarah declared that "the page of history teems with woman's wrongs" and that "it is wet with woman's tears." She asked women that they become the rightful "companions, equals and helpers" of men "in every good word and work." In her quiet way, Sarah lived out the essence of these words.

well as enough arithmetic to enable a gentlewoman to manage a large estate. A little French was important too, for French was considered the language of nobility and, like English today, was the language of communication across diverse cultures. She learned many forms of needlework and some drawing. Young ladies also were taught to sing and play the piano. Too much education for a girl beyond these essentials was frowned upon.

Yet another kind of education was reserved for the children of the South. Children of plantation owners and their slaves played as equals when they were babies and young children. At some point in their youth, however, slaveowner children learned that they owned their little playmates and could require them to do almost anything. Slave children learned that they were property, not quite people, and that if they did not obey the demands of their owners, they would be punished.

Most slaveowners accepted the unwritten rules of behavior between the races. Angelina, influenced by the strong beliefs of her sister Sarah, was never comfortable with this arrangement. She always sympathized with the slaves in the Grimké household. Against the wishes of her parents and most of her siblings, she treated slaves with kindness and respect. Even as a little girl, she would risk the wrath of her family by slipping out to the slaves' quarters at night, to comfort those who had been punished. Using oils she had collected and hidden, she would soothe the wounds of slaves who had suffered whippings or beatings.

As Angelina grew older, she became aware that people who appeared intelligent and compassionate on the surface could actually be capable of unspeakable acts of brutality. When she was thirteen years old, Angelina attended a private school for daughters of the Charleston aristocracy. The couple who ran the school were well educated and highly regarded in

Charleston, but it was their cruelty to their slaves that seared itself into Angelina's memory. In one stark example, a slave boy, the same age as the girls in the class, was called into the classroom to open a window. Angelina later recalled that his "head had been shaved in order to disgrace him, and he had been so dreadfully whipped that he could hardly walk." Angelina must have held her breath as he slowly hobbled across the room, a vision of misery. The wounds had not yet healed and were encrusted with blood and scabs. "So horrible was the impression produced upon my mind by his heart-broken countenance and crippled person that I fainted away," Angelina wrote. Later, she found out that he had recently returned from the workhouse, a place where Charleston slaveowners sent their slaves to be punished. After that vivid episode, Angelina could never walk past the workhouse without cringing. Others in her society might rationalize such abuses, but Angelina could not.

That same year, 1818, Angelina's father became very ill. The nature of his illness is unknown, save that his health declined continuously for a year. In June 1819, the family decided to send him to Philadelphia to consult Dr. Philip Synge Physick, a noted surgeon of his day. Sarah accompanied him on this journey. Dr. Physick treated Judge Grimké for two months, but could not help him. "Your father's health is in the Lord's hands," he told Sarah, and suggested that the sea air of the New Jersey shore might do the judge some good. Sarah and Judge Grimké traveled to the resort town of Long Branch, New Jersey, and took some rooms at a hotel there. But Judge Grimké's condition worsened; he died in Long Branch in August 1819, with only Sarah by his side.

Sarah returned to Philadelphia, where she remained for several months after the judge's death, then came home to Charleston, a changed person at age twenty-seven. She had stayed with Quakers while in Philadelphia. The simplicity of their lives and their abhorrence of slavery attracted Sarah. She saw how different life in the North was without slavery. And she liked it.

By this time the sisters' relationship, previously so close, had grown strained. Sarah was interested in religion and duty. Angelina, or Nina, as her family called her, was a popular and pretty teenager, interested in social occasions where she often commanded the limelight. Angelina enjoyed the softness of silks and satins, the delicacy of fine lace, the laughter of company, and the gaiety of dances and balls. For the only time in her life, in this short period Angelina even saw no wrong in slavery, provided that the slaves were treated well. Sarah found both slavery and the frivolous ways of her family intolerable.

Sarah had met a Quaker merchant, Israel Morris, on the return trip from Philadelphia, and she began to communicate with him about the Quaker faith. She started attending Quaker Meeting in Charleston. Eventually, she decided to move to Philadelphia and become a Quaker. Sarah was accompanied by her sister Anna and Anna's young daughter, Marianna. Anna's husband had died and she needed to augment her income. She thought of starting a school in Philadelphia, where working would be less damaging to the family's position and to her own pride. In May 1821, Sarah, Anna, and Marianna left Charleston for Philadelphia. Angelina was sixteen years old.

With Judge Grimké's death and the departure of Sarah and Anna, the dynamics of the Grimké household changed radically. Polly depended on her son Thomas to take the place of his father in managing the family finances; however, preoccupied with his own business, home, and family, Thomas could not give his younger siblings the attention a father might have. The other boys were grown and out of the house. Angelina was left with her mother and two unmarried sisters, attended by the house slaves. Even though she was the youngest in this household of women, Angelina began to dominate, imposing her will on many household dealings.

She convinced her mother to let her manage Kitty, a particularly troublesome slave. Polly "gave" Kitty to Angelina. Under Angelina's kind treatment Kitty's behavior improved, but she still fought with other slaves. To avoid conflict, Angelina made arrangements for Kitty to work for a friend of hers. This arrangement worked well, but Angelina was pained to be paid for Kitty's labor. Finally she transferred ownership back to her mother.

As she entered adulthood, Angelina's strong will and determination distinguished her from her peers. A young woman of strong morals, she refused to stand silent when faced with injustice. The logical choice in her life would be to remain in Charleston and become another Southern matron, although it is hard to imagine her a slaveowner. But over the next few years the religious fervor of the time would influence Angelina's choices and change her life in ways she could never have imagined.

# 3

# ANGELINA'S AWAKENING

Angelina's conflict with the traditional forms of religion began when she was thirteen. Challenging her parents and older siblings as always, she was again sending the Grimké household into an uproar. Like all the Grimké children, she had been baptized into the Episcopal faith as an infant. Now it was time for her to be confirmed. The bishop of the diocese visited Angelina at the Grimké house on Front Street; he explained that vows had been made for her at her baptism, and now she was expected to make these vows herself.

Always the factfinder, Angelina inquired what confirmation meant. The bishop referred her to her prayer book, and after reading about the rite, she informed him, "I cannot be confirmed, for I cannot promise what is here required."*

Amazed at her response, the bishop urged her to change her mind. He reminded her that all Episcopalians participated in confirmation, and that if she were to remain in the Church, she would have to conform. Angelina looked at him, and directly and calmly replied, "If, with my feelings and views as

---

*It is hard to determine what Angelina found so offensive about this service. In it, she would have vowed to follow the Ten Commandments, listened as the minister said prayers for the day, and then made a General Confession.

they now are, I should go through that form, it would be acting a lie. I cannot do it." And no amount of persuasion from Angelina's friends or family could induce her to change her mind.

Years after, Angelina learned that the church rector at St. Philip's Episcopal Church, to which the Grimké family belonged, warned the family that this act was an early sign of insanity. Those who later loved Angelina, however, interpreted it instead as an intimation of her adult courage and strict adherence to the dictates of her conscience.

The Episcopal church was the established faith of the high-standing families of South Carolina. Many planter families were lax about religion, however. Sermons only lasted twenty minutes on Sundays, and *still* the Charleston congregations talked through them.

In the early 1800s, the slackening in church attendance was not just restricted to Charleston, but was a national trend. Ordained ministers and lay preachers alike fought against this lessening of observance. A grass-roots religious revival movement—the Second Great Awakening—sprang up on the Kentucky frontier in the early 1800s, and like a hot wind, it swept eastward, scouring whole cities in its call back to the faith. Earlier revival movements had stressed the sinful nature of humanity. In contrast, the Second Great Awakening emphasized how an individual had the free will to embrace his or her personal salvation, as well as the power to change society for the better. These attitudes complemented the expansive national character of the time: Americans were an optimistic and forward-looking people, simultaneously building a new nation and bright personal futures.

Unlike many of their Charleston neighbors, the Grimkés

were relatively pious. Polly insisted that her children attend church with her, that they be confirmed at the appropriate age, pray privately in their rooms, and attend daily family prayer gatherings. Polly was not simply attached to the outward forms of religious expression; she truly believed that this path was the only route to personal salvation. So one can imagine her distress at her youngest daughter's refusal to be confirmed.

As the 1820s progressed, revival meetings grew common even in pleasure-loving Charleston. Preachers hoped to save souls at these meetings; and those who accepted Christ as their Savior could find peace in the certainty that their souls would be saved from hell. Indeed, Polly Grimké was "saved" in 1825, though she remained an Episcopalian.

Angelina, too, sought greater meaning in religion. She had begun to tire of Charleston society, a society, as historian Walter Fraser, Jr., described it, "that placed a premium on good looks, good companionship, bright conversation, and a rounded personality. It embraced the sparkling dilettante, avoided the solitary thinker." Charleston belles would caution each other not to show interest in books if they wished to be popular. Such warnings were challenges to Angelina. In 1826, when she was twenty-one, she began to attend services at the Third Presbyterian Church, attracted by the preaching of the Reverend Mr. McDowell. Angelina wrote to Sarah in Philadelphia, "O, my dear mother, I have joyful news to tell you. God has given me a new heart. . . . For many years I hardened my heart and would not listen to God's admonition. . . . Now I feel as if I could give up all for Christ. . . . I can be saved."

What did the Presbyterian Church hold out to Angelina? Her husband later wrote in 1879 that "Then first she saw that outward forms are no part of Christ's religion, which she saw to be an inward life,—the love of all beings, the wishing and willing of good to all, the law of love, the golden rule, impartial and universal, to be wrought out in loving acts." This was a faith Angelina could embrace. She spoke to Mr. McDowell and was welcomed into the church.

Like everything else she committed to, Angelina immediately threw herself into the activities of the Presbyterian Church. She began to teach a Sunday school class to a group of young ladies, which ultimately grew to 150 students. Throughout 1826 and 1827, she attended monthly concerts and prayer meetings, Bible classes, and morning and evening weekly prayer meetings. Under the auspices of the Presbyterian Church, she visited the sick and the poor. "I feel that I have begun a great work," she wrote to Sarah, "and must be diligent."

A true evangelist, Angelina longed to share her revelations about Christianity with all lost souls. Visiting prisons, hospitals, and the poor was not enough. Closer to home—no, at home— were the slaves, condemned to lives of drudgery and ignorance. Angelina asked her mother if she might read the Bible and discuss its meaning with the family slaves in the mornings. Not only did Polly agree, but she joined Angelina, as did her sisters Mary and Eliza. For as long as she lived in Charleston, Angelina continued these gatherings with the slaves.*

Even this was not enough. Angelina shared her growing concerns about slavery with Rev. McDowell. How could a Christian "own" another Christian? Wasn't this a sin? Originally from the North, Rev. McDowell agreed that slavery was evil, but argued that uprooting it would be disastrous for the South. He cautioned Angelina to pray and wait—but for her, "pray and work" was more likely.

---

*See the appendix for a letter written to Angelina by a slave who attended these meetings.

She approached the elders of the Presbyterian Church, asking them to formally denounce slavery as a sin. Slaveholders all, many privately admitted that they hated slavery, but publicly they advised her that when she was older, she would understand its necessity. To Angelina this was hypocrisy. She would never understand how a Christian could find it acceptable to have complete power over, to own, another. This issue added to a wedge which was beginning to come between Angelina and the Presbyterian Church.

In the fall of 1827, Sarah arrived from Philadelphia for a long visit. The sisters had grown closer as Angelina changed from an adolescent to a more serious young woman, and the old intimacy between them had resumed. For weeks Angelina had looked forward to Sarah's return. She imagined how proud Sarah would be of the way she conducted morning prayers. And when, the first morning Sarah was home, she refused to attend the family service, Angelina was devastated. Quakers were not supposed to participate in other forms of religious expression, and Sarah would not bend to suit the family, not even Angelina. Worse, she would not permit anyone to join her during her own prayers.

This event set the tone for Sarah's visit. For four months Sarah demonstrated and explained the route of humility and sacrifice to Angelina, who was finally ready to hear this preaching. Catherine Birney, an early biographer of the Grimké sisters, wrote of this period, "Self-sacrifice, self-immolation, in fact, was what Sarah taught; and, although Angelina never learned the lesson fully, she made a conscientious effort to understand and practice it."

Angelina began keeping a diary in January 1828. As if to remind herself daily of her higher purpose, she inscribed in the front of the diary, "Take heed lest there be more of Self than of Christ in the diary." Her diary reveals the radical changes in both her inner beliefs and outer practices. In the first entry Angelina disclosed that she had torn up her novels that day. (At that time, even the novels of such noteworthies as Sir Walter Scott and Samuel Richardson were considered foolish entertainment by many sober Christians.) In *her* diary entry for that day, Sarah admitted, "Perhaps I strengthened her [Angelina] a little. . . ."

The winds of change must have been blowing strongly that day, for Angelina didn't stop at the destruction of her novels. Sarah was sewing a pillow, and she and Angelina stuffed Angelina's ribbons and lace into it. In her diary Angelina continued, "A great deal of my finery, too, I have put beyond the reach of anyone [in the pillow]. I do want if I am a Christian to look like one." The sisters believed that they should not give such finery away, for that would be sanctioning sin in someone else.

At about this time, Angelina began to think that she was being prepared by God or Jesus for some great work, although she knew not what. In her diary, she wrote:

> It does appear to me [that she was destined for a higher purpose] and it has appeared to me ever since I had a hope that there was a work before me to which all my other duties and trials were only preparatory. I have no idea what it is and I may be mistaken but it does seem that if I am obedient to the still small voice of Jesus in my heart that he will lead into more difficult paths and cause me to glorify Him in a more honorable and trying work than any in which I have yet been engaged.

This feeling continued to grow within Angelina.

As 1828 progressed, Angelina's disappointment in the Presbyterian Church deepened. For one, its elders did not have

## Angelina Grimké's Diary

Angelina was a prolific diarist, and often revealed in her writings how faith in God and Jesus sustained her spiritually and guided her choices in life. In the passage crossed out (perhaps because she felt it revealed an excess of pride in her accomplishments), note how Angelina refers to the slave Kitty as a "servant." This was a common euphemism. *Courtesy of the Clements Library, University of Michigan*

the strength to denounce slavery publicly; in addition, the very bustle of ongoing activities that had first appealed to Angelina now seemed false. Led by Sarah, she grew more and more attracted to the simple ways and silent prayer of the Quakers. Of course, the Quakers' outspoken disavowal of slavery gained her respect too. In April, only two years after her wholehearted embrace of the Presbyterian Church, she wrote to her oldest friend, Elizabeth Bascom, "O how a few short months, yea weeks changes the character and feelings. How different do I now feel from what I did when my last letter was written to you. . . . I am just on the eve of leaving the Third Presbyterian Church. . . . Oh, my beloved sister, I cannot describe to you the agony of mind I suffered during such seasons. . . ."

Rev. McDowell pleaded in vain for Angelina to change her mind. The Presbyterians loved her enthusiasm and leadership. She contributed a great deal to the church, both through her actions and by virtue of her respected family name. Angelina was torn at the thought of leaving, but felt compelled to do it. "I thought the Saviour meant to bring me out of [my dear little church]," she wrote to her sister Anna in Philadelphia, "and I could weep at the bare thought of being separated from people I loved so dearly."

In March 1828 Sarah returned to Philadelphia, leaving a changed Angelina in Charleston. Now she spent many hours in her room, debating how she could leave the church to which she had been so attached. When she revealed her doubts to Rev. McDowell, he attributed them to the influence of Satan, yet this interpretation did not bring her back into the church.

Sarah sent Angelina Quaker books from Philadelphia. She studied them carefully, then sought out the Quaker meeting-house in Charleston. What she found could not have provided a starker contrast to what she had just left.

Unlike the active Quaker communities in the North, the faith languished in Charleston. Only two old men regularly attended Quaker Meeting (as services were called) in the bare, drab meetinghouse. Silent prayer was customary at Meeting, yet Angelina discerned tension in the silence between J.K. and D.L., as Angelina referred to the men in her letters. She wrote to J.K., asking him about his relationship with D.L. He explained that he had lent money to D.L., who had never repaid him. In addition, D.L. was a slaveholder. A Quaker slaveholder! Angelina was stunned. Nevertheless, she remonstrated with J.K. to forgive his enemies. He responded by calling D.L. a heathen and Angelina a busybody. Angelina confided to Sarah, "Though it did wound my feelings, it convinced me that he needed just what I wrote, and that the pure witness within him condemned him." So much for the Quakers of Charleston!

Angelina stopped going to Meeting but continued to wear the plain dress of the Quakers. Soon Charleston society began to turn on her. "My friends tell me that I render myself ridiculous," she wrote in her diary, "and expose the Cause of Jesus to reproach on account of my plain dressing. They tell me that it is wrong to make myself so conspicuous, but the more I ponder on this subject the more I feel that I am called with a high and holy calling and that I *ought* to be peculiar and zealous of good works."

Seeking respite from the conflicts in Charleston, Angelina sailed north in July 1828 to visit Sarah and Anna in Philadelphia. She stayed until November, enjoying the peacefulness and novelty of her surroundings. In Philadelphia her antislavery views were strengthened when Sarah's friends closely questioned her about slavery in the South. She returned to Charleston with hopes of convincing her family to renounce slavery. But hope disintegrated soon after her arrival. "My soul

Five generations of a Beaufort, South Carolina, slave family pose for a photographer in 1862. Families such as this probably worked on the Grimké plantations. What distinguished the American slave system from many others across time was that in the United States, slavery was hereditary. *Courtesy of the Library of Congress, LC-B8171-152-A*

is sorrowful and my heart bleeds. I am ready to exclaim, When shall I be released from this land of slavery? But if my suffering for those poor creatures can at all ameliorate their condition . . . I can now bless the Lord that my labor is not all in vain."

Now there were daily conflicts with family members over their luxurious lifestyle or their use of slaves. When her mother redecorated the drawing room and invited some friends to tea,

Angelina declined to come down from her room and join them. In her diary, she criticized Polly for professing to be a Christian but squandering riches. For her part, Polly complained "that she was weary of being continually blamed about everything she did." Angelina concluded, "Mother is perfectly blind as to the miserable manner in which she brought us up."

Angelina criticized her mother constantly for her treatment of the house slaves, especially Polly's personal slave, Cindie. Although Cindie was married and her relationship with her husband was a loving one, she was not allowed to spend nights with him. Rather, she slept on a pallet at the foot of Polly's bed, in case Polly should need her at night. Polly saw nothing wrong in keeping Cindie from her spouse.

It distressed Angelina to witness her family's treatment of slave children, too. Often, on winter nights, a slave child was required to sit in the cold stairwell all evening, while the family gathered in the warm drawing room (houses did not have central heating then, and individual rooms were heated by fire-places). Sometimes falling asleep in exhaustion, the child had to wait to be called to perform some odd task—perhaps bringing someone some water, or snuffing the candles, or being sent on an errand from one room to another. It did not occur to Grimké family members to do these things for themselves, and when Angelina suggested it, they were appalled.

Worst, however, were Angelina's conflicts with her brother Henry, who had moved back home to establish a male presence in the house. Her favorite brother next to Thomas, Henry was often very kind, but also had a violent temper. He frequently beat his personal servant, John. During such attacks, Angelina retired to her room to pray and write agitated entries in her diary. Once John ran away when threatened with a whipping. At first Angelina just wept over John's condition, commenting in her diary, "It seemed as though that was all I could do." But then she thought she might "tenderly remonstrate" with Henry. "I sought strength, and was willing to do so," she wrote. Angelina steeled herself and entered Henry's room, slipped her arm around him, and asked what he meant to do. Henry replied that John "deserved to be whipped until he could not stand." Angelina pointed out that that would be treating John worse than Henry treated his horse. Henry agreed, declaring that his horse was better to him than John was. The argument escalated, and Angelina finally left the room in tears. To her amazement, when John returned the next day, Henry did not punish him.

For all their disagreements, Angelina's family continued to love her and value her efforts. Forty years later, after the Civil War, her sister Eliza recalled that even though she thought Angelina's views "irrational," her sense of duty, her self-sacrifice, and her moral courage were so absolute that "she seemed to us at home like one inspired" and "we all looked upon her with a feeling of awe."

By the fall of 1829 a year had passed since Angelina first visited Philadelphia. Originally, she had planned to "act on slavery where it was . . . to act directly upon it by example, testimony, and personal effort." Yet, if she looked back, she might have wondered what, if anything, she had accomplished. She had convinced no one in Charleston to renounce slavery, and living there as a witness to slavery was agony for her.

Polly and Angelina fought constantly, Angelina wanting to change her mother's ideas about slaves. Finally, when Angelina mentioned moving to Philadelphia, Polly did not protest. Several weeks later Angelina recorded in her diary a "very satisfactory conversation" with her mother. "I found her views far more correct than I had supposed," Angelina wrote, "and I do believe that, through suffering, the great work will yet be accomplished." Polly admitted that she believed that the Lord had given her Sarah and Angelina to teach her; she concluded by saying that she saw things very differently than she had in the past. This conversation seemed to release Angelina from what she had viewed as her responsibility in Charleston. Although she had not convinced her mother to free her slaves, at least she had induced her to begin thinking about the slavery system.

She decided to move north to Philadelphia, joining Sarah in the quiet pursuits of a Quaker's life. She left Charleston in November 1829. Angelina was twenty-four. She did not know it at the time, but she would never see her mother or Charleston again.

# ❦4❧

# "Be Still"

Unlike the superhighways of today, no roads, not even dirt roads, led directly from Charleston to Philadelphia in 1829. For a trip that today might take a traveler one day by road, Angelina boarded the steamship the *Langdon Cheves*, to make the rough journey of several days on the Atlantic Ocean. Those wave-tossed days punctuated the great space between her old and new lives, and allowed her an opportunity to examine her past and anticipate her future.

Angelina was thrilled and relieved to return to Philadelphia. Of course, Sarah was there, with her deep affection and support for Angelina's transformation. Angelina's widowed sister Anna also lived in Philadelphia, with her daughter Marianna. In addition to the presence of her sisters, Angelina loved the North itself—the neat brick houses, the trees reflecting the seasons, the snow, the crisp air. She savored the independence of shopping for herself and going to the bank by herself. But most of all she loved the absence of slavery. Free black workers earned wages for themselves, not for an owner.

Both Angelina and Sarah lived on the interest from the modest inheritance each had received after their father's death. For years Sarah had lived with Catherine Morris, a well-to-do spinster who was an elder of Arch Street Meeting. Catherine and Sarah were members of the Orthodox faction of Quakers. Angelina joined Sarah in Catherine's home. Here, unlike her home in Charleston, peace and order reigned. Angelina alternated living at Catherine's and her sister Anna's homes, paying for her expenses at either house. Respectable women did not, could not, live by themselves.

Although the Society of Friends (the Quakers)* barely subsisted in Charleston, it formed a large segment of Philadelphia's population, for William Penn had established Pennsylvania as a haven for Quakers. Instead of the sneers and snickers she had endured in Charleston when walking down the street in her Quaker garb, Angelina was just one more respectable woman in Philadelphia. The freedom of this anonymity was exhilarating.

Quaker practices distinguished this group from all others. They spoke differently, using the "old way" of addressing people as *thee* and *thou*. Their calendar was different. Because the names of the months and days of our calendar were based on Norse and Roman names—pagan names—the Quakers renamed them First Month, Third Day, and so on. They intentionally made their outward appearances severely simple, so as to emphasize the all-importance of the inner, spiritual life. And the Friends' behavior set them off from other people, as they cultivated nonviolence and peaceful ways in all dealings.

Quakers also believed it was unhealthy for a congregation to be "led" by a minister with formal training; thus Quaker ministers rose from within the congregation and spoke at

---

* The Quakers were formally called the Religious Society of Friends. It is popularly assumed that the word *Quaker* was bestowed upon them because they shook during worship. However, the name originated when George Fox, the group's founder, told a judge before whom he was on trial to "tremble at the word of the Lord." The judge scornfully called the group Quakers in response.

A Quaker woman preaches at meeting. The Quakers' affirmation of women's spiritual equality was a significant factor in the birth of the concept of women's rights. Notice that men and women sit separately here, however. From *Mothers of Feminism: The Story of Quaker Women in America* by Margaret Hope Bacon. *Courtesy of the Friends General Conference*

Meeting when, seemingly, God chose to speak through them. Over time a Friend would come to be recognized as a minister by virtue of the power of his or her words. Unlike other Christian denominations of the time, the Society of Friends accorded women spiritual equality. Women, therefore, could be ministers just as men were.

Both Sarah and Angelina felt drawn to this calling. In fact, Sarah had been preparing for the ministry for years, but she had received little encouragement from the elders of her Meeting. She was a poor public speaker in Meeting, often hesitating painfully between words or rushing her words together. The other Quaker congregants interpreted this indecision and nervousness as an effort to recall statements she had tried to memorize. For the Quakers, this was a grave offense, since words in Meeting must be spontaneous outpourings from the God within oneself. Sarah denied planning or memorizing her words, but her denials were met with suspicion by the elders. While these doubts lacerated Sarah's tender heart, they angered and appalled the spirit of her younger sister.

Angelina still considered the ministry a possible goal, despite Sarah's problems. While waiting for full acceptance as a member of the Quakers, she devoted herself with typical fervor to the prescribed activities of the Arch Street Meeting House. Angelina visited the Arch Street Prison regularly and held prayer meetings there. She tended the sick and gave to the poor.

Angelina also adhered to the restrictions of Quaker social life, shunning attendance at the theater, dances, or sports events. She cultivated friendships with other young women at the Women's Meeting of Arch Street Center. And she began to receive attention from young gentlemen (Quaker, of course) seeking a wife. The most serious of these was Edward Bettle, whose parents were highly respected members of the Quaker community. Edward began calling regularly in the spring of 1831. Angelina recalled this relationship in a separate diary:

> E.B. began to visit me in such a way as induced me to believe he designed to win my affection if he could. . . . I had always respected him and soon became attracted toward him, having in earnest prayer first inquired after the Master's [God's] will and believing He had put his seal on it.

Yet despite the opportunities and activities, Angelina soon began to chafe under the inconsistencies and constraints of Quaker practices. Quakers were supposed to live simply, but Angelina could not help noticing the wealth and power of many Orthodox Quakers; was this hypocrisy? Then, Angelina was criticized for sewing fur on the inside of her bonnet; the elders thought she was trying to show off, and would not accept her explanation that, as a Southerner, she was bitterly cold in the northern winters. Quaker reading material was highly restricted too, for many Quakers believed it harmful to be too involved in the affairs of the world. In deference to this requirement, Angelina read only the Orthodox Quaker paper *The Friend*, whose articles ranged from condemnations of the Hicksites, another Quaker sect, and interpretations of the Bible, to essays on anatomy, biology, and the like. Angelina missed knowing what was happening in the nation. In the beginning of 1830, she poured out her doubts to her diary:

> I have been led to doubt if it was right for me ever to have worn the dress of a Quaker, for I despised the very form in my heart, and have felt it a disgrace to have adopted it, so empty have the people seemed to me. . . . My heart has been full of rebellion, and I have even dared to think it hard that I should have to bear the burdens of a people I did not, could not, love.

Even Quakers, Angelina was finding, were not perfect.

Perhaps Angelina would have found more kindred spirits in the more liberal sect of the Quakers, the Hicksites (so called because they were followers of Elias Hicks). The Society of Friends had split in 1828, just one year before Angelina moved to Philadelphia. The Orthodox sect, to which Angelina and Sarah belonged, was more conservative in outlook and practices. Unlike the Hicksites, they believed in greater authority of the elders to dictate behavior; they did not believe that Quakers should involve themselves in antislavery activities. When Sarah originally joined the Quakers, the split had not yet occurred. Because her friends were Orthodox Quakers, Sarah, and then Angelina, affiliated with that group.

Still seeking her calling, her purpose in life, Angelina grew interested in teaching. She was not, however, attracted to teaching in a "dame school," a school run by a woman in her home, such as the school her sister Anna operated. Angelina had heard of a training school for women founded by Catharine Beecher, daughter of the famous Presbyterian minister Lyman Beecher. Catharine had opened the Female Seminary in Hartford, Connecticut, in 1827. It was dedicated to two ideals, unusual for the time: that females were intellectually able to pursue and succeed in academic studies; and that women could make useful contributions to society outside of the home.

Angelina wrote to Catharine Beecher, declaring that she knew nothing and wished to attend school. The two met in Philadelphia in 1831, and Catharine invited her to visit the Hartford Seminary. Angelina eagerly agreed. In July 1831 she and a Quaker friend (identified only as "S" in Angelina's diary) boarded a stagecoach to make the four-day trip to Hartford.

If the journey was difficult, hot, dusty, and uncomfortable, you wouldn't know it from reading Angelina's diary account. It resonates with the joy of a person who might have just been released from prison, as if she hadn't smelled fresh air or seen the sun for months. She marveled at everything—the air, the people, the landscape. Her love of nature, and her ability to find a moral lesson in every occasion, are apparent in her description of a waterfall in the Catskill Mountains.

> I was left alone and could enjoy in perfect silence the sublimity of the scene; silence save the rushing noise of the tumbling foaming cataract. . . . I rose and began the toilsome journey up the steep and rugged hill; it is narrow, thought I, just like the way of life, too narrow to admit of help from any human arm. Here is a trial of my individual strength, and I must stand or fall alone.

Catharine welcomed Angelina warmly. She spent a week at the school, quickly fitting into its routine. She attended morning classes from 9:00 A.M. until 1:00 P.M., then afternoon classes beginning at 2:00 P.M. Angelina approved of the curriculum, which offered more rigorous studies than those of other female seminaries. She also enjoyed the acquaintance of Catharine's younger sister Harriet (who, twenty years later, became famous as Harriet Beecher Stowe, author of *Uncle Tom's Cabin*, the antislavery book that rocked the nation). After testing Angelina, Catharine said that within six months she could prepare Angelina for teaching. Angelina was satisfied with the visit and left, intending to return to Hartford soon to commence serious studies.

Back in Philadelphia she found the Quaker elders disturbed and disappointed by her sudden departure and future plans. She should have requested permission to make the trip in the first place. And no, they did *not* approve of her going to Hartford; living among Presbyterians would endanger all the progress she had made toward finding peace for her soul. How could she be so flighty? How could she desert her charities and her sisters?

If Angelina were to remain a Quaker, she would need her Meeting's approval to move to another city. She must choose: the Quakers or Hartford. She couldn't have both. Angelina struggled with her feelings of rebellion against the Friends' stifling repression. Close friends, including Edward Bettle, stopped visiting her, shunning her before she even made up her mind. Finally, Angelina decided to heed the Quaker admonishment to "be still," and she abandoned the plan to attend Hartford Seminary. In her diary she noted, "[T]ho' it had been right in me to go to Hartford, it was wrong for me to have yielded my mind up to going back, for that this was not required and that every *unrequired offering* is an *unhallowed one.* Obedience is better than sacrifice." To the modern reader, this statement sounds like a justification of actions that Angelina didn't really believe in with her whole heart.

Yet Angelina did not entirely relinquish her pursuit of an education. In the evenings she and Anna concentrated on studying history, chemistry, algebra, geometry, and arithmetic. She became interested in nutrition, and attended lectures on health and temperance given by Sylvester Graham. She even tried working in an Infant School, but confessed in a letter to Sarah, who was then visiting Charleston, "I went constantly for two weeks, but have believed this was designed to convince me that school keeping was not my business. . . . I was truly glad of a release."

In January 1832, Edward Bettle began calling on Angelina again. All through that winter and spring, Angelina wrote about the relationship in her diary. She even moved to her sister Anna's house to allow for more privacy when Edward visited. They seemed to be getting serious about each other, although words of marriage had not yet been spoken.

Through the summer and fall of 1832, Philadelphia lay in the grip of a cholera epidemic. By the time it ended in October, over 900 people had died. One of these victims was Angelina's sweetheart, Edward Bettle. Angelina turned to Edward's parents for solace, but they coldly informed her that she was neither welcome to mourn with them nor to attend his funeral. Losing Edward was painful enough; the Bettles' rejection pierced her deeply.

Angelina's move to the North, begun with such high expectations and a longing for fulfillment, had, by 1833, degenerated into a frustrating and hopeless routine. Where Sarah submitted to the Quaker restrictions, convinced she was sinful and in need of reproof, Angelina felt continually thwarted by Quaker confines. Disappointed in the faith, in the people, and in love, Angelina was prepared to seek fulfillment beyond the Quaker community.

# ❡5❡

# A CAUSE WORTH
# DYING FOR

As Angelina grew disillusioned with the "narrow, busy life" of the Friends in the early 1830s, she became increasingly aware of dramatic developments in the antislavery movement. Knowing the Quaker beliefs against slavery, Angelina had anticipated high standards against its practice among Quakers. She found to her disgust that many Quakers, while owning no slaves themselves, had no compunctions about doing business with slaveowners. This in effect supported the practice and extension of slavery.

The antislavery movement had actually been started by members of the Society of Friends nearly 150 years earlier. In 1688 in Germantown, Pennsylvania, Quakers exhorted fellow Friends to free their slaves. "To bring men hither, or to rob and sell them against their will, we stand against," the Germantown Quakers wrote. Because the Friends believed in making decisions by consensus, however, they moved no faster than their most conservative members. As a result, antislavery as a Quaker movement progressed very slowly through the 1700s.

The legal ramifications of slavery were debated by lawmakers as early as the 1780s, when the Constitutional Convention met and hammered out the Three-Fifths Compromise in the Constitution (Article I, Section I, Clause 3), stating that, for the purpose of apportioning state representation, "all other persons" would be counted as three-fifths of a free person. Yet not all blacks in the United States, even in the South, were slaves. Free blacks lived marginal lives in both the North and the South. Some had been freed; some were the children of slaves; in the North, some had escaped from slavery and begun new lives. In the South the movements of free blacks were severely restricted. While life was better for them in the North, prejudice was still rampant and they were second-class citizens. In most states they did not have the right to vote, for example. Nor did they have the same job or educational opportunities, with rare exceptions.

Most white people were uncomfortable with the presence of free blacks; particularly in the South, whites feared that free blacks represented to slaves the possibility of freedom. The question was: What should be done with these people? In 1816, a group composed almost entirely of Southerners established the American Society for Colonizing the Free People of Colour of the United States. This group proposed a solution for the problem of free blacks, whom most whites, even Northerners, viewed as a nuisance and a disturbance. The original goal of colonization societies was to send free blacks back to Africa to set up their own colonies and governments, having experienced the "benefits of Western civilization." The country of Liberia was founded in 1822 for this express purpose. Colonization grew in popularity, first as a method of dealing with free blacks, and then as a way to end slavery gradually. It was supported by many Southerners as well as Northerners; indeed, of the 130 antislavery societies in the United States in 1827, 106 of them were in Southern states. The vast majority of these accepted colonization as the best method for dealing with blacks, whether free or slave.

Few blacks, however, were interested in returning to Africa; most had been born in the United States and felt that this was their home. Blacks saw colonization as an attempt to avoid a very difficult problem. One free black bitterly explained, "[T]he colonizationists want us to go to Liberia if we will; if we won't go there, we may go to hell."

The early 1830s witnessed the emergence of a new breed of antislavery activists, who supported black opposition to colonization. These reformers, called abolitionists, advocated the *complete and immediate emancipation of slaves throughout the South—indeed, throughout the world.* By "immediate," they meant that the process of emancipation should begin immediately, not that all slaves should be freed immediately, without any support (although people often misinterpreted their goal as a result of their choice of this word). One of their most famous—or infamous, as he was in the South—leaders was William Lloyd Garrison, who began publication of the abolitionist newspaper *The Liberator* on January 1, 1831. In it he gave supporters of slavery notice of his intentions: "I am in earnest; I will not equivocate; I will not excuse; I will not retreat a single inch—AND I WILL BE HEARD."

Garrison and his like made Southerners feel defensive about their practices and fearful of the consequences. What would happen to the Southern way of life if the slaves were freed? How would slaves react if they heard these radical ideas? Then, just eight months after the first issue of *The Liberator* was published, the Southerners' greatest fear was realized. In Southampton County, Virginia, Nat Turner led a group of seventy fellow slaves on a rampage for four days, killing fifty-seven white men, women, and children. Within two months the insurrectionists had been captured and hung, but Nat Turner's rebellion sent shock waves of terror

**William Lloyd Garrison**
devoted his life to the abolitionist
cause. Mild and gentle in private
life, Garrison saved his bite for his
public persona. He once wrote,
"The compact which exists between
the North and the South is a
covenant with death and an agree-
ment with hell." Garrison was
Angelina's exact contemporary:
They were born and died in the
same years.

reverberating throughout the South. In many places in the
South, particularly on large plantations, blacks significantly
outnumbered whites. Would more slaves throw off their
shackles and rise against their owners? Such fears were very
real in 1831.

In reaction to Nat Turner's rebellion, the state legislature of
Virginia began to debate "what to do about slavery" in
December 1831. Even Angelina, isolated from most news, was
aware of this event, and she wrote to Sarah, who was visiting
Charleston, "Didst thou know that great efforts are making in
the House of Delegates in Virginia to abolish slavery?" Despite
what Angelina had heard, immediate emancipation, such as
abolitionists proposed, was not even a consideration. The majority of the legislators wanted to deport all blacks, but no one

could offer a plan to offset the cost of liberation. What compensation would planters get for slaves? Who would pay for transport to Africa? Instead, the legislature took no action. Rarely, if ever again, was the issue of freeing the slaves discussed in a Southern legislature.

The following year, an argument over national tariffs galvanized the citizens of South Carolina into declaring their right to nullify, or not follow, federal laws that favored one region of the United States over another. The Nullification Crisis foreshadowed the Secession Crisis which led to the Civil War. This earlier crisis was resolved when President Andrew Jackson threatened to use force to make South Carolina comply with federal law on the one hand, but also lowered the tariff on the other. Charlestonians who opposed nullification and supported the Union were led by none other than Thomas Smith Grimké, Angelina's beloved brother. In a prophetic letter, Angelina wrote to Thomas of her fears for the future:

> I may be deceived, but the cloud which has risen in the South will, I fear, spread over all our heavens, though it looks now so small. It will come down upon us in a storm which will beat our government to pieces. . . . We may boast of this temple of liberty, but oh, my brother, it is not of God.

Angelina's interest in the slavery question continued to grow. In the spring of 1833 she asked Thomas to send her more information on the principles of colonization. "You Southerners have no idea," she wrote, "of the excitement existing at the North on the subjects of abolition and colonization."

Later that year, after a great Parliamentary debate that was closely watched in the United States, the British Empire outlawed slavery in its colonies in the West Indies. Like a pistol at the start of a race, this act inspired the formation of the American Anti-Slavery Society. This group united three main forces within the abolition movement. One contingent, the New York Anti-Slavery Society, was a strong, well-organized group, led by notables such as Joshua Leavitt, Elizur Wright, and the philanthropic Tappan brothers, Lewis and Arthur. The second contingent, the Western movement, had its roots in Ohio, where it had made spectacular gains "abolitionizing" thousands of people. Through Theodore Weld and his converts, this group had strong connections with the New York group. Lastly, operating in comparative isolation were the Garrisonians in Massachusetts. Garrison's aggressive tone in *The Liberator* made him the scourge of Southern planters but also gave people the misguided impression that he led the national organization.

The American Anti-Slavery Society differed in aim and method from the colonization societies that preceded it. In its constitution, this nationwide organization proclaimed that its primary objective was "the entire Abolition of Slavery in the United States," but not "by resorting to physical force"; thus it would work through nonviolent means. Another feature that distinguished the American Anti-Slavery Society was its insistence on the equality of blacks and whites in all aspects of life. Instead of freeing slaves and sending them to Africa as the colonizationists proposed, abolitionists wanted to begin immediate planning for the slaves' emancipation. They envisioned slaves passing through a period of preliminary citizenship, training, and education before gaining complete freedom. Abolitionists were firmly rooted in the revivalism of the Second Great Awakening. They believed that they were doing the work of God; indeed, many had been preachers before heeding this new calling.

The first meeting of the American Anti-Slavery Society took place on December 4, 1833, in Philadelphia. Just a few days later, led by the Hicksite Quaker Lucretia Mott, the Philadelphia Female Anti-Slavery Society was formed, the first of its kind in the United States. Although Sarah and Angelina must have learned about these groups, and were undoubtedly interested, there is no evidence that either sister considered herself an active participant at this time.

In February 1834 yet another great tale of abolitionist fervor swept the hearts and imaginations of those who despised slavery. The young men attending Lane Theological Seminary in Cincinnati, Ohio, staged an eighteen-day-long series of debates, discussing the merits of colonization versus immediate abolition. Leading these debates was the idealistic Theodore Weld, so passionate about this issue he had vowed never to marry until slavery was abolished. By the end of the debates, nearly the entire campus, which had been predominantly colonizationist, had converted to abolitionism. Not content with theorizing, the young men went out into Cincinnati's black community, organizing schools and various social services for their black brothers and sisters.

Afraid that the school's benefactors would cut funding, the trustees of Lane Seminary demanded that the students halt their abolitionist activities. In a precursor to future student-led free-speech revolts, the "Lane rebels" refused. Threatened with expulsion, fifty-one of the ninety students resigned from the seminary. Some entered Oberlin College in Ohio, thus jump-starting traditions that would place Oberlin in the forefront of movements for freedom and equality. Others, like the famous Weld, became agents—speakers—for the American Anti-Slavery Society, preaching the evils of slavery to all who would listen.

The events at Lane Seminary were widely published and inspired many people to join the abolitionist cause. Years later Angelina told Theodore Weld that his words and deeds had so greatly thrilled her that just to hear his name was to feel herself moved. We know that Angelina was reading antislavery material in 1834 because the sisters discussed the movement when their brother Thomas passed through Philadelphia in September. Thomas's interests extended beyond the law profession to education reform, the peace movement, and politics. He had come north to speak on education before the College of Professional Teachers in Cincinnati. He also planned to visit their brother Frederick while in Ohio. Angelina had not seen Thomas for five years. The sisters discussed with him their growing interest in abolition. Thomas asked them to gather antislavery literature for him, and promised to give the subject due consideration. Sadly, however, Thomas died of cholera while in Ohio.

By 1835 Angelina had become a regular reader of the antislavery newspapers. Most of her Quaker friends viewed her developing interest in abolition with cold disapproval. Quakers did not own slaves and frowned upon slavery, but the Orthodox among them believed that Quakers should distance themselves from worldly affairs. Focusing on a topic such as abolition would lead one away from a spiritual focus. Many Quakers were also uncomfortable with the notoriety of the abolitionists and thought Quakers should avoid associating with them. Angelina chose to ignore these feelings and admonitions. The walls of her Quaker existence continued to crumble.

Angelina began attending antislavery meetings, despite warnings from Sarah and Quaker elders. Sarah observed, years later, that Angelina had "found to her surprise that their [abolitionists'] principles were her principles, and that [abolitionists] were men and women with whom she could work for the slave." On March 3, 1835, Angelina attended a lecture by the noted British abolitionist George Thompson, an incendiary speaker. He typically preached on such topics as the corruption of slavery; how, contrary to what slaveowners said, slavery was not supported by the Bible; and how the British West Indies now thrived under a free system.

The word *lecture* makes the event sound quite tame, but the aftereffects of antislavery lectures were anything but tranquil. Thompson's speeches in other cities had resulted in riots, not because he encouraged them (he did not), but because the topics of slavery and emancipation were such sore spots in American society. Many white people, Northerners as well as Southerners, were prejudiced against blacks. Many felt that freeing the slaves would stir up trouble and that the abolitionists deserved to be met with violence. A riot in Philadelphia in 1834, targeting first abolitionists but then blacks, left forty-five black homes destroyed and one person dead.

Angelina sympathized with the abolitionists, convinced they were victims of an ignorant and violent populace. In May 1835 she confided in her diary for the first time in five months:

> I have become deeply interested in the subject of abolition. I had long regarded this cause as utterly hopeless, but since I have examined anti-slavery principles, I find them so full of the power of truth, that I am confident not many years will roll by before the horrible traffic in human beings will be destroyed in this land of Gospel privileges. . . . My earnest prayers have been poured out that the Lord would be pleased to permit me to be instrumental of good to these degraded, oppressed, and suffering fellow-creatures. Truly, I often feel ready to go

to prison or to death in this cause of justice, mercy, and love; and I do fully believe if I am called to return to Carolina, it will not be long before I shall suffer persecution of some kind or other.

Wherever the abolitionists spoke there was sure to be dissension, and often violence. The summer of 1835 was marked by ugly snarls against blacks and abolitionists. In July, another anti-black riot blistered through Philadelphia. In *The Liberator* William Lloyd Garrison wrote an appeal to the citizens of Boston, describing the difficulties and persecution suffered by abolitionists. In August, the papers carried news of yet another riot, this time in Angelina's home city of Charleston. Rumors had flown through the city regarding a shipment of abolitionist literature that had arrived in the post office. A crowd forced its way into the post office and burned the "incendiary" literature. The mob hung effigies of Garrison and other antislavery leaders. Angelina must have wondered which of her friends and relatives were part of that crowd. Philadelphia. Charleston. What was next?

In an attempt to clear her mind of the dramatic happenings of the past few months, Angelina left Philadelphia. She went to find peace at the home of her friends Margaret and James Parker in the little coastal town of Shrewsbury, New Jersey, just a few miles from Long Branch, where her father lay buried. Angelina did not read any abolitionist literature during her weeks in Shrewsbury. Yet she could think of nothing else, and the question "What can I do? What can I do?" ran through her mind continuously. She kept thinking of Garrison's appeal for a fair hearing. She finally determined to write him a letter, although she had never met him. For a woman to write a personal letter to a man she did not know was considered a brazen act at that time.

Angelina began the letter by reviewing her response to the recent proslavery riots:

I can hardly express to thee the deep and solemn interest with which I have viewed the violent proceedings of the last few weeks. Although I expected opposition [to abolition], yet I was not prepared for it so soon—it took me by surprise, and I greatly feared Abolitionists would be driven back in the first onset.

Angelina was inspired to find that Garrison did not retreat in the face of such opposition.

The ground upon which you stand is holy ground: never—never surrender it. If you surrender it, the hope of the slave is extinguished. . . .

She compared the abolitionists to the martyrs of old, who also were persecuted for their beliefs. And then she identified herself with the cause of abolition.

If persecution is the means which God has ordained for the accomplishment of this great end, EMANCIPATION, then . . . I feel as if I could say, LET IT COME; for it is my deep, solemn, deliberate conviction, that *this is a cause worth dying for.* . . .*

Occasionally one can look back on a life and determine a specific moment that was a turning point, or a point of no return. For Angelina Grimké, this letter was most assuredly that moment.

At first she thought that just writing the letter would be a sufficient release for her. But then, for days, she deliberated about whether to send it. Later, explaining to Sarah how the letter came into Garrison's hands, she wrote, "I implored

---

*See the appendix for the full text of Angelina's letter to William Lloyd Garrison.

This is the masthead of the most influential antislavery periodical before the Civil War, although the circulation of *The Liberator* was never more than 3,000 subscriptions annually. Ironically, it was Southerners who increased the newspaper's notoriety by reprinting its articles and attempting to refute them. From Dumond, *Antislavery Origins of the Civil War in the United States*

Divine direction, and next morning, after again praying over it, I felt easy to send it, and, after committing it to the [mail], felt anxiety removed, and as though I had nothing more to do with it." Angelina didn't think that Garrison would publish the letter, but even if he did, she thought that he would not use her name. But he did publish the letter and he did use her name, for even in the North, the Grimké name carried much weight. Indeed, upon receipt of the letter, Garrison wrote to a friend, "Angelina E. Grimké, sister of the [late] lamented [Thomas Smith] Grimké, has sent me a soul-thrilling epistle."

The letter was less than soul-thrilling to the Quakers of Angelina and Sarah's Meeting. A few weeks after Angelina sent the letter, Friend Bettle, Quaker elder and father of Edward Bettle, came calling. He angrily showed her *The Liberator* with her letter printed in it. "He was most exceedingly tried at my having written it," Angelina recalled in her diary, "and also at its publication." The Friends wanted Angelina to write to Garrison, expressing disapproval at the letter's publication, and asking him to withdraw it. This, Angelina refused to do. "I . . . said I felt willing to bear any suffering," she wrote in her diary, "if it was only made instrumental of good."

At that time, it was thought that a lady's name should appear in print only three times—at birth, at marriage, and at death. It was unseemly for a lady's letter to be published and read by all. Sarah was distressed with Angelina, who in turn felt terrible about causing pain and disgrace to her family. "Nevertheless," she concluded, "I could not blame the publication of the letter, nor would I have recalled it if I could."

Angelina Emily Grimké had found her voice. On August 30, 1835, she wrote a letter that changed her life. It would change her sister's as well, for Sarah ultimately joined Angelina in her crusade against slavery. But more than that were the lives of American slaves and women, which would never be the same for the work Angelina Grimké would do on their behalf.

# ❧6❧

# ABOLITION
# WOMEN

On the surface, Angelina's life seemed to return to normal in the fall of 1835. She was back in Philadelphia, and the blasts of wrath evoked by her letter in *The Liberator* had faded.

But beneath the surface, Angelina's mind was focused almost exclusively on abolition. She read everything about antislavery that she could get her hands on. She began writing articles for antislavery publications. She also began acting on her antislavery beliefs. When she and Sarah learned that their mother was making her will, they asked Polly to include her slaves in her bequests to them, so that they could eventually be freed. To this Polly agreed.

Through the Philadelphia Female Anti-Slavery Society, Angelina became involved in the Free Produce movement, an effort to boycott slave-made products. Several Quaker women had opened Free Produce stores, which sold only products that did not use slave labor. Buying only Free Produce appealed greatly to Angelina and Sarah, for whom every act was a moral statement. Even though the cotton was of inferior quality and the sugar, which came from beets, was coarse and brown, the sisters continued to use only Free Produce until the end of the Civil War.

In the Philadelphia Female Anti-Slavery Society, Angelina met many like-minded women. Lucretia Mott was a Hicksite minister and highly thought of among her fellow Quakers. Abba Alcott was the wife of the innovative teacher and transcendentalist thinker Bronson Alcott, and mother of Louisa May Alcott, who later wrote *Little Women*. Angelina also developed friendships with black women active in the society: Harriet Purvis, whose husband Robert was a well-known leader of the black community; Charlotte, Sarah, and Marguerite Forten, daughters of shipbuilder James Forten; Grace Douglass and her daughter Sarah.

These ties with black women opened the Grimké sisters' eyes to the prejudice endured daily by Philadelphia's free blacks, who made up more than 10 percent of the city's population. Sarah and Angelina discussed this prejudice with their black friends. They noticed that even in Quaker meetinghouses, a separate bench was reserved for blacks, often in some undesirable location, such as beneath the stairs. Angelina and Sarah spoke out against such outrages. The following year, they would take their places with their black friends on those benches. From then on, they always sat with the black population wherever they encountered segregation.

In February 1836, Angelina and Sarah attended the Quaker Yearly Meeting in Providence, Rhode Island. Once again, upon leaving Philadelphia, Angelina was struck by an almost overwhelming sense of freedom and release. Even Sarah commented on how much easier it was for her to be a Quaker minister away from "that city of bonds and afflictions." She also warmed more toward the abolitionist movement. In Rhode Island, Angelina was welcomed as a near-celebrity because of her letter to Garrison. The free and frequent discussions of slavery with people in Rhode Island were like a balm to her spirit.

The sisters realized that they were no longer comfortable

living in Catherine Morris's home because of their change in attitude regarding abolition. But where to go? It was not easy to find acceptable arrangements. For a while Sarah stayed with their friend Jane Smith and her widowed mother, but there really was not enough room in Jane's home. Sarah stayed with friends in Burlington, New Jersey, during the summer of 1836, while Angelina returned to the Parker home in Shrewsbury, where she had spent the previous summer.

Margaret Parker remembered how distracted Angelina had been that second summer. She was consumed by the issue of slavery. Angelina would often say such things as, "Is there nothing I can do? The churches all seem drugged to death." One evening after they'd gone to bed, Angelina's distress reached a crisis level. Mrs. Parker could hear her sobbing in her room for hours. When she went in to comfort Angelina, she found her lying on the carpet, "her face buried in a pillow." Angelina apologized profusely for having disturbed her host, and they parted. But in the morning, Angelina's look and step revealed that the crisis had passed. "It has all come to me," Angelina said. "I will write an 'Appeal to the Christian Women of the South.'" She began work that day and wrote steadily for two weeks.

Angelina began her Appeal by declaring to Southern women, "It is because I feel a deep and tender interest in your present and eternal welfare that I am willing thus publicly to address you." She leaned heavily upon interpretation of the Bible to illustrate the wrongs of slavery. With characteristic logic she argued, "Are you willing to enslave *your* children? You start back with horror and indignation at such a question. But why, if slavery is *no wrong* to those upon whom it is imposed?"

To her Southern sisters who might reply to these arguments, "Well, what can we do? We are only women and have no power to make or change laws," Angelina replied,

*"You are the wives and mothers, the sisters and daughters
of those who [make the laws]; and if you really suppose
you can do nothing to overthrow slavery, you are
greatly mistaken.* You can do much in every way: four
things I will name. 1st. You can read on this subject. 2d.
You can pray over this subject. 3d. You can speak on
this subject. 4th. You can act on this subject."

Angelina suggested such actions as emancipating their own
slaves or teaching their slaves to read and write.

Later in the Appeal, Angelina justified the actions of abolitionists, insisting on their nonviolent approach but warning
Southerners that now all the dark secrets of slavery would be
revealed. She also discussed the problem of racial prejudice in
the North, wondering how people who treated other people so
ignobly could call themselves Christians.

While working on the Appeal, Angelina received a letter
from Elizur Wright, secretary of the American Anti-Slavery
Society. He invited her to speak to women's groups in New York
about her experience of slavery. It was a shocking idea, an elec-
trifying idea. For a woman to speak in public, even to other
women and in the privacy of a home, was highly unusual.
Angelina wrote to Sarah, asking her opinion. Sarah perhaps
sensed that Angelina was growing apart from her; she responded that she was willing to give up her "precious child" if
Angelina felt it was right to go. Angelina replied, "Elizur
Wright's letter threw my mind into such a state of deep suffer-

---

Opposite: The American Anti-Slavery Almanac brought the abolitionist message
into the home at a time when almanacs were as common in households as Bibles.
Theodore Weld prepared the almanacs for the Society in the years 1839 to 1841. In
addition to the usual almanac information about sunrise, sunset, and the tides,
these contained antislavery stories and principles, and facts and arguments against
slavery. The cover of this almanac criticizes the fugitive slave laws in the North.
From Dumond, *Antislavery Origins of the Civil War in the United States*

—VOL. 1. No. 4.—

# THE
# AMERICAN
# ANTI-SLAVERY
# ALMANAC,

FOR

# 1839,

BEING THE THIRD AFTER BISSEXTILE OR LEAP-YEAR, AND THE
63D OF AMERICAN INDEPENDENCE.   CALCULATED FOR
BOSTON ; ADAPTED TO THE NEW ENGLAND STATES.

What has the North to do with Slavery ?

" Have no *fellowship* with the unfruitful works of darkness, but rather *reprove* them. "

## NEW YORK & BOSTON:

PUBLISHED FOR THE AMERICAN ANTI-SLAVERY SOCIETY.

NEW YORK : — S. W. BENEDICT, 143, NASSAU ST.

BOSTON : — ISAAC KNAPP, 25, CORNHILL.

ing the night previous that I hardly slept at all. The bare idea that such a thing may be required is truly alarming, and that thy mind should be at all resigned to it increases the fear I feel that probably I may have to do it."

To Mr. Wright she explained that such a venture would have to wait until she was done writing her Appeal. Would the American Anti-Slavery Society be interested in seeing it? Yes, he answered, they would. When it was done she mailed it off to New York, and after reading it, Elizur Wright responded, "I have just finished reading your Appeal, and not with a dry eye. . . . Oh that it could be rained down into every parlor in our land." The American Anti-Slavery Society printed and distributed the thirty-six-page pamphlet, which quickly became a mainstay of abolitionist literature in the North.

In the South it was another story. Copies of the Appeal that were sent by mail to South Carolina were publicly burned by postmasters. Angelina and Sarah had thought of returning to South Carolina that winter to spend time with their family. Hearing of this plan, the mayor of Charleston came to Polly's house and informed her that he could not vouch for Angelina's safety, and so she would not be allowed to enter the city. If she did, she would be arrested and put on the first steamship heading north. Angelina's friends wrote to her, begging her not to put her life in danger. She replied that because of her concern for her family, not fear for her life, she would not come. Angelina had been banned from Charleston. She and Sarah never went home again.

At the same time that Angelina was finishing her Appeal, Sarah's life was changing too. The Quaker elders had treated her worse and worse as the years progressed. "Oh! The cruel treatment I have undergone from those in authority," she wrote. "I could not have believed it had I not been called to endure it." On August 3, 1836, Sarah attended the Orange Street Meeting. She was speaking when Jonathan Evans, a respected elder who presided over the Pennsylvania Yearly Meeting, interrupted her: "I hope the Friend will now be satisfied." Today this would translate into "Shut up," and for a Quaker to make such a remark in Meeting was more than a rebuke—it was a vile insult. For Sarah it was the final blow. "Surely," she wrote in her diary, "the feelings that could prompt to so cruel an act cannot be the feelings of Christian love. But it seems to be one more evidence that my dear Saviour designs to bring me out of this place." She determined to leave Philadelphia forever.

Angelina continued to reflect on the Quakers' stifling effect on her, too. Two days before Sarah's encounter with Jonathan Evans, Angelina had written to her, "I sometimes feel frightened to think of how long I was standing idle in the marketplace, and cannot help attributing it in a great measure to the doctrine of nothingness so constantly preached up in our Society." After Sarah's encounter with Jonathan Evans, she joined Angelina in Shrewsbury, where the two pondered their futures.

Angelina was now determined to take up the Anti-Slavery Society's invitation to speak in New York. Although Sarah had grown to appreciate the abolitionists much more over the past year, she still could not decide whether to join her sister. Then she received a letter from Polly, who was looking out for her daughters' welfare from a great distance. Sarah recalled, "Her [Polly's] maternal feelings were aroused at the prospect of Angelina's going on such a mission alone, and she entreated me to accompany her. It was like a voice from the Lord, and I instantly resolved to do so." From then on, save for one year during the 1850s, the sisters would travel together, work together, spend their lives together.

And so in October 1836, Angelina and Sarah Grimké, two unmarried Southern women, traveled to New York City to speak to other women about slavery. They worked as agents of the American Anti-Slavery Society, but they refused to accept any wages, choosing instead to use the small income from their inheritance to cover expenses.

The antislavery movement had grown immensely over the past few years. By 1835 there were between 400 and 500 abolition societies; the year 1835 alone saw the formation of 328 groups. Now the majority of groups were in the North, not the South; they were abolitionist, not colonizationist. Abolitionist leaders had found that the most effective way of reaching people was not by flooding the countryside with publications, but by addressing people directly, as Theodore Weld had done at Lane Seminary and throughout Ohio.

In the fall of 1836 the American Anti-Slavery Society carefully planned and organized a campaign to strike a mortal blow at slavery. They gathered together forty selected agents and provided them with a three-week intensive training session. Then, just as the biblical apostles had done, the agents would go forth and spread the gospel of abolition. To their number were added two women, Angelina and Sarah Grimké. As women and as Southerners from a wealthy slaveholding family, they offered a unique perspective.

The training sessions lasted eight hours a day, from nine in the morning to one, three to five, and seven to nine at night. Yet in a letter to Jane Smith, Angelina confided that she and Sarah "never feel weary *at all*. It is *better*, far better, than any Yearly Meeting I ever sat." The men attending the convention treated the sisters with complete respect and also complete equality.

For the first time they had as much right to speak, to question, even to object as the men.

In fact, these men were a far cry from the narrow-minded Philadelphia Quakers Angelina and Sarah had deserted. Cultured, self-effacing, and dedicated to the cause of abolition, many had worked for the Society since its beginning. Arthur and Lewis Tappan were wealthy merchants; John Greenleaf Whittier was a Quaker and a poet; Henry B. Stanton and Gerrit Smith were nationally known speakers.

But the man whom both sisters admired most was Theodore Weld. Nicknamed "the most mobbed man in America," he had taught many other agents both the techniques of public speaking and the logical arguments that were the underpinnings of abolitionist rhetoric. Weld edited the American Anti-Slavery Society's publication, *The Emancipator*. Over the next few years, he would write or edit many of the Society's publications, including *The Power of Congress Over Slavery in the District of Columbia* (1836), *The Bible Against Slavery* (1837), and *Emancipation in the West Indies* (1837). Originally a preacher, Weld had ruined his voice by speaking out relentlessly against slavery and was no longer able to speak in public. But he could, and did, speak to the agents at the training convention.

In writing to her friend Jane Smith, Angelina relayed, "Today [November 11] we enjoyed a moral and intellectual feast in a most noble speech from T. D. Weld, of more than two hours, on the question, 'What is slavery?' I never heard so grand and beautiful an exposition of the dignity and nobility of man in my life." William Lloyd Garrison, also present, introduced the sisters to Weld after his speech, and in the same letter, Angelina continued with a description of Weld. "Perhaps now thou wilt want [to] know how this lion of the tribe of

# THEODORE DWIGHT WELD

Theodore Weld was descended from a long line of New England clergymen. Possessed with almost limitless energy, he was running a 100-acre farm by the time he was fifteen. But he wanted an education and attended several colleges. Before he became an abolitionist speaker, he campaigned for temperance, was a Presbyterian revivalist, and worked for the manual labor movement, whereby college students paid part of their expenses by working at school.

Weld was a man of vast contradictions. Slovenly in appearance, he was nevertheless scrupulously clean, bathing daily in cold water. He was one of the most powerful revivalist preachers and abolitionist speakers of his time, yet he liked nothing more than romping with young children: "I *must cut capers*," he confessed in a letter to his betrothed wife in 1838. Fierce as a lion when dealing with pro-slavery viewpoints, he was kind and gentle with any suffering being. Perhaps these seeming contradictions were what endeared him to his students when he taught later in life; in his collected letters are scores of notes from former students thanking him for his beneficial influence.

Abolition *looks*. Well, at first sight there was nothing remarkable to me in his appearance and I wondered whether he really was as great as I had heard. But as soon as his countenance became animated by speaking, I found it was one which portrayed the noblest qualities of the heart and head, beaming with intelligence, benevolence, and frankness."

In December Angelina and Sarah began their New York speaking tour. By then, Sarah had resolved not just to accompany Angelina, but to speak as well. From the numbers of women expressing interest in such talks, it was clear that private parlors would be vastly insufficient as venues. When the Reverend Mr. Dunbar, a Baptist minister, offered a meeting room in his church as a place to speak, Angelina commented, "We both felt that this was just the right thing." December 16 was set and publicized as the date. Both Angelina and Sarah grew very nervous as the day approached, but were comforted by their faith in God and the support of abolitionists such as Gerrit Smith and Theodore Weld.

Even today people get nervous speaking in public for the first time. In 1836, it was noteworthy enough for a woman to speak for moral reform in the parlor of another woman. When the meeting was moved to a church, it became public speaking, and that was approaching the scandalous. *Women simply did not do that!* It was outside of their designated sphere—the home; it exposed them to the barbs of anyone who chose to enter the room; and to many, it suggested that the "weaker sex" was trying to assume the role of the stronger. When Angelina began speaking in public, her intention was not to flaunt the conventions of society. She was willing to speak publicly only to bring to light the sufferings of the slave, to contribute in any way possible to the eradication of slavery.

At 3:00 P.M. on December 16, three hundred women came to

hear the sisters' historic presentation. The opening prayer was said by Rev. Henry Ludlow of the Spring Street Presbyterian Church, at whose home the sisters were guests and who accompanied the sisters to the meeting. Then Rev. Ludlow and Rev. Dunbar left, for it was considered inappropriate for ladies to speak in the presence of the opposite sex. In a letter to Jane Smith written the next day, Angelina recounted, "I spoke for about forty minutes, I think, feeling perfectly unembarrassed, after which Dear Sister did her part better than I did." The meeting ended at 5:00 P.M., with the ladies agreeing enthusiastically to meet again soon.

Afterward, Angelina and Sarah had tea at the home of Lewis Tappan. Theodore Weld was there, "all anxiety to know about [the meeting]." Tappan's daughter Juliana, who had attended the talk, mentioned that a man had tried to listen at the back of the room but had been escorted out by Rev. Ludlow. At that, Angelina wrote to Jane Smith, "Weld's countenance was instantly lighted up, and he exclaimed how extremely ridiculous to think of a man's being shouldered out of a meeting for fear he should hear a woman speak." And at that, Angelina and Sarah smiled and said that they "did not know how it seemed to others, but it looked *very strange* in [their] eyes. . . ."

Angelina and Sarah began to speak on a regular basis at the Spring Street Presbyterian Church. Their talks grew so popular that soon all the women who attended could not fit in the meeting room. So they adjourned to the church proper, and the sisters spoke *from the pulpit*—another recorded first in American history.

Speaking in public was often difficult for Angelina. In January 1837 she wrote, "I can truly say that the day that I have to speak is always a day of suffering. . . ." Yet by February

Angelina was growing more comfortable in her role as speaker. She had been criticized for moving around too freely when she spoke; people thought women should be still. "But," Angelina countered, "I think the more a speaker can yield himself [sic] entirely to the native impulses of feeling, the better, and this is just what I do."

In a remarkably openhearted letter to Jane Smith written on January 20, 1837, Angelina revealed a multitude of feelings about speaking in public.

> Thou mayest remark I speak of our *talks* as *lectures*. Well, this is the name that *others* have given our poor effort, and I don't know in fact what to call such novel proceedings. How little! how *very little* I supposed, when I used to say, "I wish I was a *man*, that I might go out and lecture," that *I* would ever do such a thing. The idea never crossed my mind that *as a woman* such work could possibly be assigned me. But the Lord is "wonderful in counsel, excellent in working," making a way for his people when there seems to be *no* way. Dear Jane, I love the work. I count myself greatly favored in being called to it. . . .

When Angelina and Sarah first came to New York at the close of 1836, the American Anti-Slavery Society discussed plans with them to establish a national abolition organization for women. After their speaking tour was underway, the Grimké sisters contributed to the effort to launch that group by meeting regularly with the New York women's antislavery society. The American Female Anti-Slavery Society's first national convention was set for May in New York City.

Angelina was disturbed to see that no black women were present at meetings of the New York women's group. To Jane Smith she wrote on April 3, 1837, "The Lady's [Anti-Slavery]

Society is . . . utterly inefficient and must continue so until our Sisters here are willing to give up sinful prejudice. It is a canker worm among them and paralyzes every effort. They are doing *literally nothing* as a Society for the colored people." Angelina and Sarah pressed their abolitionist sisters in New York to face their own prejudice and urged black friends in Philadelphia to attend the national convention.

Angelina also mentioned to Jane Smith that they had met the previous week with a group of black people in a black church in Poughkeepsie, New York. For the first time in her life Angelina spoke to a "promiscuous" assembly, that is, men and women mixed. "I found that the men were no more to me then, than the women," she remarked diffidently. To many people in 1837, however, such events were an abomination, proving beyond a doubt that abolition women wanted to be men, take the place of men, or rule over men.

The first convention of the American Female Anti-Slavery Society was held in May. Seventy-one delegates attended the convention, with Angelina and Sarah representing South Carolina. Lucretia Mott was there, along with a large contingent of Philadelphians. Many women came from Massachusetts, where female antislavery groups were strong. Angelina was impressed with the organizational skills of Boston delegates such as Maria Weston Chapman, Mary S. Parker, Lydia Maria Child, and Anne Warren Weston. The Grimké sisters introduced several resolutions to the convention. According to historian Gerda Lerner, their most significant contribution was "their insistence that race prejudice must be fought in the North as well as the South."

The convention also focused on the one political action allowed to women, the right of petition, guaranteed in the First Amendment of the Bill of Rights. In 1835 abolition societies

had begun flooding Congress with petitions to abolish slavery. Southern Congressmen responded by passing a "gag rule," forbidding any petitions regarding slavery to be brought to the attention of the House of Representatives, although congressmen with antislavery sympathies could still receive these petitions. Abolitionists and others were incensed by this limitation on free speech. The American Female Anti-Slavery Society resolved to fight the gag rule and gather even more signatures from thousands of women across the North. Ironically, the Southerners' effort to squelch free discussion about slavery only kindled the Northerners' political quest for freedom and equality. Discussions were heated. Sympathy for the abolitionists grew.

The women's convention also released a new treatise by Angelina, "An Appeal to the Women of Nominally Free States." This publication pointed out that the North was free only in name, because of its economic involvement with the South and its acceptance of the South's "peculiar institution." Women *had* to be concerned about slavery, Angelina asserted:

> The denial of our duty to act in this case is a denial of
> our right to act; and if we have no right to act, then may
> we well be termed "the white slaves of the North," for
> like our brethren in bonds, we must seal our lips in si-
> lence and despair.

This comparison of women to slaves hinted at the next milestone that Angelina and Sarah would reach, when they began their speaking tour in Massachusetts just a few weeks after the convention ended.

# ❦7❧

# ANGELINA OR DEVILINA?

Sarah and Angelina arrived in Boston late in May 1837. Angelina, age thirty-two, had lived in the North for over seven years; Sarah, at age forty-four, had lived there for sixteen years. Almost immediately upon arriving in Boston, the sisters entered into a whirl of antislavery conventions and meetings. They were much impressed with the Boston Female Anti-Slavery Society. The Boston women were experienced in running their own affairs and in taking leadership roles in the antislavery movement. At the convention in New York, Sarah and Angelina had learned much from them about organizing and running meetings.

The Boston women had earned a reputation for toughness in the face of danger. When Garrison was almost lynched in 1835, the mob that attacked him had first broken up a meeting of the Boston Female Anti-Slavery Society. Angelina called Maria Weston Chapman, leader of the Boston women, "one of the noblest women I ever saw." Married to a Boston merchant, Maria brought wealth, prestige, and an uncompromising attitude to the organization. She edited the society's annual reports, with the aid of her sister, Anne Warren Weston. Angelina also befriended Lydia Maria Child, whose career as a children's author came to a halt in 1833, when she published

This woodcut was adopted by the American Anti-Slavery Society as a logo or emblem, and often appeared on their stationary and publications. A companion woodcut showed a male slave kneeling and in chains, with the caption, not surprisingly, "Am I Not a Man and a Brother?" From Bourne, *Slavery Illustrated in Its Effects Upon Women*

the antislavery tract *An Appeal in Favor of That Class of Americans Called Africans.* After that, her popularity plummeted and publishers refused to print her books.

At antislavery meetings in Boston, discussion often centered on the role of women in the abolition movement. At one meeting, Angelina found both men and women suggesting that "it was time our [women's] fetters were broken. . . . Indeed very many seem to think that a new order of things is very desirable in this respect."

Angelina was well aware that a woman speaking out could hurt both the abolition movement and the budding cause of woman's rights, and that her own role could be pivotal in both these areas. To her friend Jane Smith, she revealed her innermost concerns:

> I feel as if it is not the cause of the slave only which we plead, but the cause of woman as a responsible moral being, and I am ready to exclaim, "Who is sufficient

for these things?" These holy causes must be injured if
they are not helped by us. What an untrodden path we
have entered upon! Sometimes I feel almost bewildered,
amazed, confounded and wonder by what strange con-
catenation of events I came to be where I am and what
I am. And if I look forward, I am not less bewildered. I
see not to what point, all these things are leading me.
I wonder whether I shall make shipwreck of the
faith—I cannot tell. . . .

It was her belief in God's guidance, Angelina concluded, that
enabled her to continue on this "untrodden path."

Angelina compared Boston favorably to other Northern
cities she'd lived in; "there is real anti-slavery here: a heart to
work, a tongue to speak. We feel ourselves surrounded by an
elastic atmosphere which yields to the stroke of the wings of
effort. . . . In New York we were allowed to sit down and do
nothing. Here, invitations to labor pour in from all sides. . . ."

And labor they did. Their first lecture took place on June 6
in Dorchester. The day before, Angelina wrote to Jane, "Pray
for us, dear Jane. We need it more than ever. We see only in a
glass darkly what results are to grow out of this experiment."
Despite Angelina's apprehensions, the meeting went well.
Originally it was to have been held in a private house, but
when 150 women showed up, it was adjourned to a public hall
instead.

Afterward the sisters drove to Quincy to visit ex-president
John Quincy Adams, now a member of the House of
Representatives and leader of the antislavery petition campaign
in Congress. If the sisters expected to convert this aged cam-
paigner for justice to the principles of radical abolitionism,
they were disappointed. However, when Angelina asked
Adams "whether women could do any thing in the abolition of

Slavery," he smilingly responded, "If it is abolished, they must do it." In just three years Adams himself would strike a massive blow against slavery by arguing—and winning—the *Amistad* slave revolt case before the United States Supreme Court.

The next few weeks were a whirlwind of meetings. The sisters traveled by coach from one town to the next, trying to reach as many listeners as possible. On June 7 they spoke in Boston; 400 attended. On June 8, they spoke in Brookline; 75 attended. June 9 found them in North Weymouth; 120 attended. By June 23, over a period of eighteen days, they had held eleven meetings and spoken to over 3,500 people.

The sisters were a "sensation," as historian Gilbert Barnes has put it. Many who came because they were curious left as converts to the abolitionist cause. Rev. Robert Wallcutt, who worked with Garrison in the office of *The Liberator*, recalled in 1879, "Angelina, especially, possessed a rare gift of eloquence, a calm power of persuasion, a magnetic influence over those that listened to her, which carried conviction to hearts that nothing before had reached."

As the lectures progressed, the sisters established a pattern in their speaking. Angelina dealt with the moral and religious questions about slavery, while Sarah handled legal concerns. Sarah gracefully accepted Angelina's more powerful speaking presence. For her part, Angelina praised Sarah's speaking at every opportunity.

The sisters were aided in their tour by Henry C. Wright (no relation to Elizur Wright), an agent of the American Anti-Slavery Society who worked in Massachusetts. Brother Wright, as they called him, organized their tour, traveling ahead to find places to speak and places for them to stay.

It was not easy to speak to large groups of people in the nineteenth century. There were no microphones to augment the human voice, no air conditioning to cool the air in the heat of summer, no automobiles to whisk one from place to place. Add to that the discomfort of traveling in a woman's long and cumbersome garb. The sisters generally stayed in the homes of antislavery leaders in the community where they were speaking; they usually did not have the luxury of privacy afforded by the typical hotel or motel room of today. Yet for both sisters, working for the end of slavery was far more important than any physical inconvenience. They didn't complain.

Before the end of the first week of the tour, they found themselves speaking to "mixed" audiences. In North Weymouth on June 9, "nearly 30 men [were] present. Pretty easy to speak," Angelina noted. On June 19 in Boston, fifty men attended Sarah and Angelina's lecture. Their first large mixed audience assembled at Lynn on June 21, when over one thousand people attended, about half of them men. Angelina's only comment was, "Great openness to hear and ease in speaking."

Not everyone was as matter-of-fact about these revolutionary events. Strong opposition followed hard on the heels of the Grimkés' speaking tour. Most Americans had fixed beliefs about the sphere of women. By their actions, the Grimké sisters took the first steps toward revealing the true condition of women in the early nineteenth century. More than the vote was at issue. Legally, for example, a married woman sacrificed not just her surname, but her property and many legal rights as well. Educationally, the number of female seminaries, while growing, was still pitifully small; and the education was often inferior to that received by men. The jobs available to women after completing this education were severely limited in scope; women had yet to "break into" the professions of law, medicine, and college teaching, for instance. A working woman could expect to earn less than half the salary of a man for the same work. Even in organized religion, there was prejudice against women stepping beyond strictly prescribed boundaries.

Hostility to the sisters speaking in public, to mixed groups, about abolition seemed to come from all quarters—from the press, from church groups, and even from old friends. Critics drew on ancient and revered sources. In the New Testament, for example, the apostle Paul said, "Let a woman learn in silence in all submission. And I do not permit a woman to teach, or to have authority over a man, but to be in silence" (I Timothy, ii, 11–12). Could a statement restricting women be more clear? Why were these sisters speaking out in direct defiance? Angelina and Sarah answered these critics, drawing on biblical sources as well, but to little avail.

For the press in New England, it was open season on the sisters. In August 1837, the *Boston Morning Post* reprinted this snide remark from a New Hampshire paper:

> Why are all the old hens abolitionists? Because not being able to obtain husbands they think they may stand some chance for a negro, if they can only make amalgamation fashionable.

Ten days later the same newspaper attacked Angelina and Sarah directly:

> The Misses Grimké have made speeches, wrote pamphlets, exhibited themselves in public, etc., for a long time, but have not found husbands yet. We suspect that they would prefer white children to black under certain circumstances, after all.

Some editors began calling Angelina "Devilina" instead.

These attacks revealed some common biases with regard to "woman's place." A woman's place was in the home. Her husband was supreme, family came next, and her own needs and

AN AMALGAMATION POLKA.

Those who feared equality between blacks and whites were terrified that such associations would lead to race wars or to amalgamation, the mixing of races. This 1845 lithograph by E. W. Clay reflects and satirizes that fear. *Courtesy of the Print Collection, Miriam and Ira D. Wallach Division of Art, Prints and Photographs, The New York Public Library. Astor, Lenox and Tilden Foundations*

desires were a distant third. For most people at that time, a woman who did not marry therefore had no place. (Remember that Sarah and Angelina, as respectable women, could not live by themselves when they moved from their mother's house.) Both sisters knew intuitively that women, whether married or not, had more to offer society than homemaking talents. Just as men did, women should have the right to choose whether to marry, without criticism from society.

In addition, the vicious references to amalgamation, the mixing of the races, insinuated that the Grimkés were looking for black husbands because no white man wanted to marry them. This gross distortion of the sisters' motives only shows the vulgar brutality of those who made the gibes. The Grimkés' efforts were to free slaves, not to find husbands, as anyone who attended their lectures would know.

Just ten years earlier, Angelina had been living in a culture where a slur to a woman's reputation was just cause for a duel between two gentlemen. It must have been particularly painful for the sisters to suffer such attacks on their honor. Their courage in continuing to expose themselves for an unpopular cause shows the strength of their beliefs and their character. They jeopardized their honor for abolition's sake.

Yet another salvo was fired when Angelina's old friend, Catharine Beecher, published her book *Essay on Slavery and Abolitionism with reference to the Duty of American Females*. The book was addressed specifically to Angelina Grimké and was written in response to Angelina's "Appeal to the Christian Women of the South" of 1836. In it Beecher defended the colonization movement; colonizationists believed in freeing the slaves gradually and sending them back to Africa. She also defended the concepts that women should be subordinate to men and that women had no business in any public sphere of the antislavery movement—speaking, writing, even petitioning. Today it may seem ironic that a woman such as Catharine Beecher, who promoted education for women, would take such a stand. In the 1830s, however, Beecher's position was both more prevalent and more acceptable than Angelina's.

Angelina did not bend meekly to Catharine's criticisms. As she traveled on her lecture tour, she wrote letters in response to every accusation. These letters were originally printed in *The Liberator*. She wrote thirteen letters in all, ten dealing with abolition, two with woman's rights, and the final letter, a conclusion.

To Jane Smith, Angelina commented, "I have not spared her [Catharine Beecher] at all as thou wilt perceive. . . . I do not know how I shall find language strong enough to expose my indignation at the view she takes of woman's character and duty." The following year, with the help of Theodore Weld, Angelina revised the letters and compiled them into a book, published under the title *Letters to Catherine E. Beecher in Reply to an Essay on Slavery and Abolitionism Addressed to A. E. Grimké*.

Indeed, Angelina did not spare Catharine Beecher. In her letter on immediate emancipation, Angelina wrote:

> Dost thou ask what I mean by emancipation? I will explain myself in a few words. 1. It is "to reject with indignation, the wild and guilty phantasy, that any man can hold *property* in man." 2. To pay the laborer his hire, for he is worthy of it. 3. No longer to deny him the right of marriage, but to "let every man have his own wife, and let every woman have her own husband," as saith the apostle. 4. To let the parents have their own children, for they are the gift of the Lord to *them*, and no one else has any right to them. 5. No longer to withhold the advantages of education and the privilege of reading the bible. 6. To put the slave under the protection of equitable laws.

Angelina continued:

> Now, why should not *all* this be done immediately? Which of these things is to be done next year, and which the year after? and so on. *Our* immediate emancipation means, doing justice and loving mercy *to-day*— and this is what we call upon every slaveholder to do.
>    I have seen too much of slavery to be a gradualist. . . .

In Angelina's letter defending woman as a moral being, she supported a woman's right to petition:

The right of petition is the only political right that women have: why not let them exercise it when they are aggrieved? Our fathers waged a bloody conflict with England, because *they* were taxed without being represented. This is just what unmarried women of property are.

Angelina defended woman as man's equal in every respect:

I affirm, that woman never was given to man. She was created, like him, in the image of God, and crowned with glory and honor; created only a little lower than the angels,—not, as is almost universally assumed, a little lower than man. . . .

Even more damaging than Catharine Beecher's essay was the response of church sects to Angelina's and Sarah's speaking tour. The Yearly Meeting of Friends in Rhode Island, so welcoming only a year earlier, in 1837 closed Quaker meetinghouses to antislavery lecturers. Church leaders wanted to squelch the dissension that antislavery was causing among Quakers.

Now, Quakers were a minority in New England, and their disapproval, while saddening to the Grimkés, was of little real consequence. In contrast, the Congregationalists formed the major Protestant sect in New England, the offspring of the Puritan tradition. Congregational churches provided their communities with a central forum for discussion. When they expressed reservations about abolitionists in general, and women abolitionists in particular, the world that was New England stopped to listen.

An association of Congregational ministers issued a letter attacking abolitionists. This became known as the infamous Pastoral Letter. Ministers read the letter to their congregations in early July; on July 12 it was printed in the *New England*

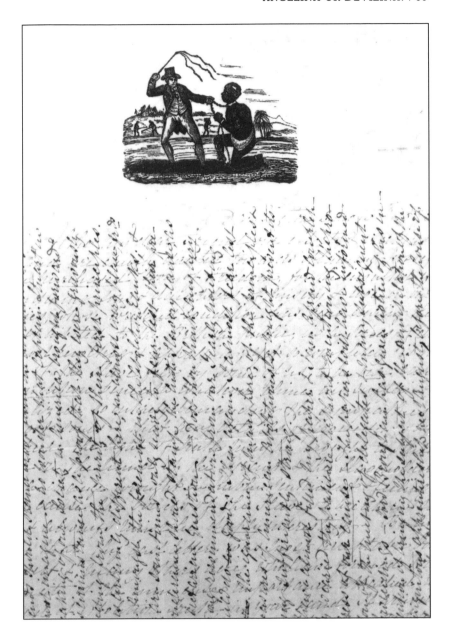

The English abolitionist Elisabeth Pease wrote this letter to Angelina on February 13, 1838. She used a method called "cross-hatching," common to the prolific letter writers of the time as a way of saving paper. Notice the abolitionist woodcut at the top of the page. *Courtesy of the Clements Library, University of Michigan*

*Spectator.* The first aim of the letter was to forbid Congregational ministers to allow their churches to be used as meeting places by abolitionists; but it also aimed to re-establish the subordinate position of women in society:

> The power of woman is in her dependence, flowing from the consciousness of the weakness which God has given her for her protection. . . . But when she assumes the place and tone of man as a public reformer, she yields the power which God has given her for protection, and her character becomes unnatural.

The Letter warned, in a memorable metaphor,

> If the vine, whose strength and beauty is to lean upon the trellis and half conceal its clusters, thinks to assume the independence and the overshading nature of the elm, it will not only cease to bear fruit, but fall in shame and dishonor into the dust.

This not-so-subtle reference to the Grimké sisters' speaking tour was lost on no one. Sarah, who had been writing a series of letters to the *New England Spectator* on the position of women, added repudiation of the Pastoral Letter to her responses. These letters were subsequently published as the historic book *Letters on the Equality of the Sexes and the Condition of Women* (1838). For her part, Angelina practically exulted to Jane Smith:

> The whole land seems roused to discussion on the *province of woman*, and I am glad of it. We [Sarah and I] are willing to bear the brunt of the storm, if we can only be the means of making a breach in that wall of public opinion which lies right in the way of woman's true dignity, honor and usefulness. . . . [M]any of our New England sisters are ready to receive these strange doctrines. . . . What dost thou think of some of *them walking* 2, 4, 6 and 8 miles to attend our meetings?

But it would be false to suggest that all this criticism was insignificant to Angelina and Sarah. The sisters were not sure how to proceed. In truth, Angelina never really spoke about *woman's rights* when she lectured—but she always dealt with *woman's moral responsibility*. Sarah, on the other hand, did "preach up women's rights most nobly and fearlessly," as Angelina proudly wrote. The Boston Female Anti-Slavery Society supported Angelina's and Sarah's writing about woman's rights. The New York antislavery women, however, were not as clear about what was appropriate. Lewis Tappan's daughter Juliana wrote to Anne Weston, "On the one hand, we are in danger of servile submission to the opinions of the other sex, and on the other hand, in perhaps equal danger of losing that modesty, and instinctive delicacy of feeling, which our Creator has given as a safeguard to protect us from dangers . . . . How difficult it is to ascertain what duty is, when we consult the stereotyped opinions of the world. . . ."

Angelina and Sarah looked for guidance to the antislavery leaders whom they most trusted and respected—Theodore Weld and William Lloyd Garrison. Weld worked at the national office of the American Anti-Slavery Society in New York, and the sisters communicated with him by letter. He tried to convince Angelina and Sarah that they and the movement would be best served if they ignored the verbal slings and just went on speaking for antislavery, *but not for woman's rights*. Weld, and many others in the national antislavery society, were very worried that the "woman question," as it came to be called, would overshadow the issue of slavery. The American Anti-Slavery Society's goal was to convert as many people as possible to abolitionism. Anything that hampered that effort was expendable to them.

In August, the Quaker poet John Greenleaf Whittier wrote to Angelina and Sarah, asking them not to write or speak about woman's rights: "Is it not forgetting the great and dreadful wrongs of the slave in a selfish crusade against some paltry grievance of our own?" Weld echoed these sentiments: "Let us *first* wake up the nation to lift millions of slaves of both sexes from the dust . . . and then . . . it will be an easy matter to take millions of females from their knees and set them on their feet. . . ."

To these arguments Angelina hotly replied that it was the Pastoral Letter, not Sarah's letters, that had aroused New England to the subject of woman's rights. She continued:

> [T]his invasion of our rights was just such an attack upon *us,* as that made upon Abolitionists generally when they were told a few years ago that *they had no right* to discuss the subject of Slavery. . . . *The time* to assert a right is *the* time when *that* right is denied. *We must establish this right* for if we do not, it will be impossible for *us* to go *on with the work of Emancipation.*

William Lloyd Garrison, leader of the Boston contingent of the antislavery movement, provided a counterpoint to the advice of Weld and Whittier. Garrison encouraged the sisters to speak and write as they wished. He supported woman's rights in *The Liberator*, but he also supported many other doctrines which even today would be considered quite radical. For instance, Garrison published articles charging that the United States government and the U.S. Constitution were immoral for supporting slavery. He encouraged people not to vote or participate in the political process. He vilified the established churches for their acceptance of slavery. Garrison and his followers offended many mainstream Americans. Other leaders of the American Anti-Slavery Society were concerned that Garrisonians would make it impossible for abolition ever to become a major interest of Northerners.

As if things weren't confusing enough, Henry Wright, who aided the Grimké sisters' tour in Massachusetts, published an article in *The Liberator* which gave a misleading image of their tour. He made it sound as if the sisters were emphasizing abolition and woman's rights equally in their lectures. In fact, Angelina never spoke about woman's rights in her lectures, although as a woman lecturing she stimulated thought about these rights. Wright, a Garrisonian, also had been speaking on his own, supporting such theories as no-government (that the country would be better off without any government) and anti-Sabbath doctrine (that no one day should be singled out as being particularly holy). The American Anti-Slavery Society had been frustrated for some time with Wright, who was thwarting their efforts to appeal to moderates. The article on the Grimké sisters was the final straw. The Society relieved Wright of his Massachusetts agency and transferred him to Philadelphia, where they felt he would do less harm.

The sisters despaired without him. Angelina wrote to Jane Smith, "This has been a great disappointment to us for we have been calculating upon him to go before us as a pioneer and appoint all our meetings. . . ." The tour suddenly became much more difficult, with Angelina and Sarah having to make arrangements for themselves. Because of the Pastoral Letter they found many churches closed to them. There were times when they had to speak in barns, having traveled for many hours without food or rest.

Angelina wrote to Weld, asking him whether she and Sarah were agents of the American Anti-Slavery Society. Since they had initially been invited by the Society to speak to women, they assumed that they were its agents, even if they accepted no pay. But Weld wrote back saying that he could find no document in the Executive Office establishing that as a fact; the sisters were on their own, to do as they pleased. Instead of interpreting this license as freedom, the sisters felt deserted by the American Anti-Slavery Society—and twice deserted, because now, when overwhelmed with criticism, they looked to friends for support and felt that the Society offered none. Angelina blamed Weld for "firing" Henry Wright; he claimed it was the decision of the entire Executive Committee; and they argued back and forth in letters through the late summer and early fall.

The opponents of abolitionism could not have been more satisfied with the results of the summer of 1837. The Pastoral Letter and its aftermath revealed and widened already existing cracks between the branches of the movement. And the biggest fissure by far was brought on by the woman question.

In August 1837, Sarah became ill with a cough. She rested for several weeks at the home of Samuel and Eliza Philbrick in Brookline, but the cough persisted. The weather began to turn cold, and Weld cautioned Angelina and Sarah against straining their health. "As cold weather comes on, do both of you take care of yourselves, my dear sisters. . . . You have never tried a New England autumn before." But the sisters kept speaking and the people of Massachusetts kept coming to hear them.

Then, in early November, Angelina took ill with a high fever. She insisted on speaking one last time in Hingham, but collapsed after an hour and a half, leaving the lecture unfinished. It was all Sarah could do to get her back to the Philbricks' home in Brookline, where she lay in bed for weeks with a fever that refused to go down. For a while she was so ill that she couldn't even bear to hear Sarah read letters to her from friends.

for some other man to offer to escort her home. When Sarah and Angelina left New York for Boston, Weld took them to their steamboat, but his farewell was anything but personal. For a proud spirit like Angelina's, unrequited love was a humiliating experience. She resolved not to divulge her emotions even to Sarah, with whom she normally shared everything. Instead, she would suppress her tender feelings. It would be easier with the distance from New York to Boston between Weld and herself.

Weld corresponded regularly with the sisters after their departure, however. The letters between him and Angelina reveal a warmth and gentle teasing that suggests a developing fondness. Angelina complained so much about his poor handwriting—his "scratchifications," she called them—that Weld went out and bought a new fountain pen. Weld, in turn, wrote that he could tell Angelina was a Southerner by the way she scolded him. And so on.

Yet when the woman question threatened the unity of the abolitionists, playfulness shifted to exasperation on both ends of the correspondence. The accusations grew personal. This exchange escalated and culminated in two letters from Weld to Angelina in mid-October, in which he dissected her numerous character flaws. In the first letter he wrote:

> [Y]our habits of reason greatly expose you to *fallacies*— the splendor of some grand practical *conclusion*, which you deem eminently desirable, so dazzling your eyes that you see *no* road but that which leads to it. . . .

And in the second letter:

> To KNOW and to RULE ones [sic] own spirit is the rarest and most difficult of human attainments. . . . you have studied everything more than the *moral* elements of your own spirit. . . .

It was characteristic of reformers to point out the faults of their fellow reformers, as a service toward reaching perfection. Yet perhaps Weld had gone too far. The second letter so unhinged Angelina that she read it once and could not bring herself to read it again. She responded with silence. Two weeks later, she took ill with the fever that prostrated her through the month of November.

When Weld heard that Angelina was seriously ill, he begged the sisters to put off the speaking tour until the spring, and to spend the winter in a somewhat warmer city such as Philadelphia. Angelina finally wrote to him again at the end of November, a brief note describing her illness and recovery, with no mention of the previous letters. Their correspondence resumed in a gentler if less personal tone, as if they both took several steps back from a cliff they'd been approaching at full speed.

As Angelina recuperated, she began to revise her letters to Catharine Beecher, preparing them for publication in book form. Weld offered to help her make revisions. She accepted, acknowledging, "I am a miserable hand at revision for I have too much pride to see my own faults, so please to point them out, I need not say freely as you *rejoice* in the wounds you inflict. . . ." In January, in a discussion of friendship, Angelina wrote, "and now let me tell you how often I have thanked God for such a friend as you have proved to me, one who *will* tell me my faults. . . . [Y]et, Brother, I think in some things you wronged me in *that letter never to be forgotten*."

Weld always wrote jointly to the sisters. But on February 8, he wrote a separate letter to Angelina, marked *Private*.

A paragraph in your last letter, Angelina, went *to my soul*. You feel that I have "wronged" you and think that what I said "was not written in the spirit of love". . . . [T]here are other expressions in your letter . . .

which reveal to me that the spirit and manner of my reproof have inflicted upon you ABIDING PAIN. . . . Have I indeed done this to *you* Angelina? I will not say I have not.

Weld continued:

> I would explain the mystery of the *seeming* unkindness and cruelty of my spirit toward you in reproof, did not higher considerations than *inclination* or self interest forbid me to do it, until I have *first* fulfilled an obligation which I am now convinced should have been discharged long ago—a *sacred* duty which I owed to *you*, to my own soul, and to our Father who knoweth the thoughts and intents of the heart. . . . I know it will surprise and even amaze you, Angelina, when I say to you as I now do, that for a long time, *you have had my whole heart*.

From the day he read her first letter in *The Liberator*, Weld continued, his spirit had been drawn to hers "by irrepressible affinities." But because she was a woman, he could not simply write to her without a formal introduction. He continued:

> From the time that I met you in New York to this moment in which I write, this same state of mind has continued unvarying, except that it has gathered strength with every day until long stifled convictions of duty make it impossible for me longer to refrain myself, and I now tell you the whole. . . . I cannot close this letter without announcing to you a fact, the knowledge of which may *spare you much pain*. It is this. I have *no expectation* and almost no *hope* that my feelings are in *any degree* RECIPROCATED BY YOU. . . . If (and I have hardly a hope that it is otherwise) your heart, Angelina, does not reciprocate my love, I charge you before a risen Lord not to shrink for a moment through fear of giving me pain from declaring to me the *whole truth*. . . .

Three days after receiving this letter, Angelina answered Weld:

> Your letter was indeed a great surprise, My Brother, and yet it was no surprise at all. It was a surprise because you have so mastered your feelings as never to betray them; it was no surprise because in the depths of my own heart *there was found a response* which I could not but believe was produced there by an undefinable feeling in yours. . . . You say that my letter revealed to you that you had inflicted *"abiding pain;"* Yes! you did, and it was love for you which caused reproof to sink so deep into my heart. . . . But enough of this, you have broken the precious box of ointment over my wounded spirit, and it is healed.

Angelina revealed that a letter of Theodore's printed in *The Liberator* two years earlier had also drawn *her* to *him*. "I longed to hold communion with you, but never expected the privilege." She, too, had struggled against her feelings for him after they met. "I have prayed earnestly against them at times, whilst at others I have gone to my Heavenly Father like a little child and asked Him *if* it was wrong to love you as I did; WHY He had constituted me a being imperfect, a *half* only of myself as it were; why He had created these restless longings of my heart. . . ?"

Angelina went on to chide Weld for not revealing his feelings to her. She asked,

> Do you believe that our Father ever begets such pure and holy feelings in one heart without touching the other? I *feel* my Theodore that we are the two halves of one whole, a twain one, two bodies animated by one soul and that the Lord has given us to each other.

Sarah added a note to Angelina's letter, saying that she always felt that Angelina and Theodore were kindred spirits and that she was not surprised by the revelation of their love. "You have my prayers, my love, my sympathy," she concluded.

With such declarations of love, you would think that the lovers would fly to each other at the next available moment. That was not how events unfolded for Angelina and Theodore, however. For his part, Theodore was so overwhelmed by Angelina's love that it took him days to regain control of himself. "My heart is full!" he finally wrote. "I have so long wrestled with myself like a blind giant stifling by violence all the intensities of my nature that when at last they found *vent* and your voice of love proclaimed a *deliverance* . . . all the pent up tides of my being . . . broke forth at once and spurned control."

Angelina was torn about whether to see him or not. The greatest speaking challenge of her life was scheduled for February 21, a scant two weeks after Theodore's declaration of love. "I sometimes think," she wrote to him, "that these two things together [seeing him and her upcoming lecture] will almost overpower me."

The momentous speaking engagement had started as a jest. At a meeting of the Massachusetts Anti-Slavery Society (an all-male society), members planned to present petitions decrying slavery in the District of Columbia to a committee of the Massachusetts state legislature. After the meeting, Henry B. Stanton visited Angelina and Sarah at the Philbricks' home. Jokingly, he asked Angelina if she would like to speak before the legislature, "as the names of some thousands of women were before it as signers of petitions." Why jokingly? Because no American woman had ever addressed a legislative body before; it was unthinkable.

But not unthinkable for Angelina. She considered it for several days, then sent word that she would like to do it, "if the friends of the cause thought well of it." The men in the

Massachusetts Anti-Slavery Society were against it, although in theory they supported woman's rights. Angelina then consulted the Executive Committee of the American Anti-Slavery Society; its members, all male, hemmed and hedged as they tried to decide how to respond. Ultimately Angelina resolved to speak regardless of what they thought, "for woe is unto me if I speak not." Francis Jackson, one man who did support her, secured permission for Angelina to speak from the head of the legislative committee, who happened to be his friend. Two presentation dates were set, February 21 and 23. To Jane Smith, Angelina declared, "I feel, dear, that this is the most important step I have ever been called to take—important to woman, to the slave, to my country and the world."

Sarah had planned to make the first presentation, but took ill on February 21, so Angelina spoke both times. As she climbed the steps of the State House in Boston, she could not help noticing the crowd of people who could not get seats inside to hear her speak. To Theodore she recalled, "I was never so near fainting under the tremendous pressure of feeling. My heart almost died within me. The novelty of the scene, the weight of responsibility, the ceaseless exercise of mind through which I had passed for more than a week—all together sunk me to the earth. I well nigh despaired." As in countless times before, her belief in God steadied Angelina and enabled her to continue.

The hall was packed with a thousand people, most of them men, most of them from the upper classes. Lydia Maria Child, a leader of the female abolitionists in Boston, recounted the event in a letter on March 20, 1838, to her friend Elizabeth Carpenter: "I think it was a spectacle of the greatest moral sublimity ever witnessed. The house was full to overflowing. For a moment a sense of the immense responsibility resting on her seemed almost to overwhelm her. She trembled and grew pale. But this passed quickly, and she went on to speak gloriously, strong in utter forgetfulness of herself, and in her own earnest faith—in every word she uttered. . . . I believe she made a very powerful impression on the audience."

Angelina's words rang out through the hall, gripping abolitionist and skeptic alike with their spellbinding power. "I stand before you as a southerner," she said,

> exiled from the land of my birth by the sound of the lash, and the piteous cry of the slave. I stand before you as a repentant slaveholder. I stand before you as a moral being . . . and as a moral being I feel that I owe it to the suffering slave and to the deluded master, to my country and the world, to do all I can to overturn a system of complicated crimes, built up upon the broken hearts and prostrate bodies of my countrymen in chains, and cemented by the blood and sweat and tears of my sisters in bond.*

Afterwards, the abolitionist Wendell Phillips recalled that Angelina's speech "was the profound religious experience of one who had broken out of the charmed circle, and whose intense earnestness melted all opposition. The converts she made needed no after-training. It was when you saw she was opening some secret record of her own experience that the painful silence and breathless interest told the deep effect and lasting impression her words were making."

Two days later, Angelina returned to speak to the legislative committee again. This time Sarah accompanied her but did not speak. The chairman invited Angelina to address the audience from his own lectern and Sarah was seated in his chair. Angelina reflected on the event to their friend Sarah Douglass

---

*See the appendix for more of the speech that Angelina made that day.

in Philadelphia: "What the *effect* of these meetings is to be, I know not, nor do I feel *I* have anything to do with it. This I know, that the Chairman was in tears almost the whole time that I was speaking. . . . We Abolition Women are turning the world upside down."

Angelina described the speeches to the Massachusetts legislature in great detail to Theodore as well. In the same letters, she alluded to another major speaking prospect that was in the early stages of development. The Boston Female Anti-Slavery Society was sponsoring a series of lectures by Angelina Grimké on the subject of slavery. She would present six lectures, to be given weekly at the Odeon, Boston's largest lecture hall. Angelina had spoken to groups in churches and other meeting halls, but had never given a series of formal lectures in one of America's great cities. Even greater demands were being made on Angelina.

Throughout this time Angelina and Theodore continued to write torrents to each other. They related all their faults to one another, so neither would be unpleasantly surprised. Theodore characterized himself as intolerant, sarcastic, and self-indulgent. Angelina said she was "exceedingly selfish, proud, *impatient* of contradiction and *irritable*." She considered giving Theodore up, because she feared she would be unable to make him happy. When Angelina questioned when they could meet, Theodore replied, "I must not see you till sure that I can *rule* my own spirit and God will *soon* enable me to do it."

The two discussed marriage shortly after disclosing their love for one another. For Angelina, "the *perfection* of our being is no doubt the great end of marriage." Weld viewed their impending marriage as a glorification of God. On March 12 he wrote, "We marry Angelina not *merely* nor *mainly* nor *at all comparatively to* ENJOY, but together to do and to dare, together to toil and testify and suffer, together to crucify the flesh with its afflictions and lusts and to keep ourselves and each other unspotted for the world. . . ."

The Odeon lectures were scheduled to begin just ten days later. If Weld was to come to Boston at all, it would have to be before the lectures, because the sisters would be leaving Boston shortly after the lectures concluded. He resolved to come a few days before the first lecture. He was determined to keep their engagement a secret, both to protect Angelina from intrusion into her private life and to keep the antislavery cause free of gossip and rumor. Weld tried to enter Boston as unobtrusively as possible, coming by coach through Hartford and Worcester rather than by steamship. Angelina teasingly wrote to him, "I expect no poor [fugitive] slave ever passed through our land under more suffering from fear of exposure. You did not tell me that *vanity* was among your defects, but I find to my surprise that you are so vain as to suppose that you cannot possibly even pass through Providence or Boston without the blast of wonder and rejoicing being blown on the arrival of so great a personage."

After months of waiting and reams of correspondence, the lovers were united for a few blissful days. Following Theodore's departure, Angelina reflected on the visit in a letter to him:

> We *met* with emotions too big for utterance, too deep to find any relief in tears, our aching hearts could find no vent . . . but as day by day the feeling of oppression, of smothered emotion, was gradually displaced by communion with each other and with Jesus, our souls experienced a holy calm. . . .

Over the four days they planned their wedding and resolved that Sarah should live with them too. Angelina did not want to live without Sarah, and in the 1800s such an arrangement for an unmarried sister was common. Sarah and Theodore already cared for each other as brother and sister. As Theodore wrote to Sarah, "I feel as though dear Angelina and I both greatly need your constant watchful influence and shall both be unspeakably blessed by it."

Through March and April the Odeon lectures claimed the sisters' attention. Sarah gave the first lecture at the Odeon, Angelina the rest. After Angelina's first lecture, she wrote to Weld, "My tongue was loosed, my spirit unfettered and lifted above all human feeling and I spoke (if I am any judge) with more power and authority than I ever did in Boston before." After the final lecture, Samuel Philbrick recorded in his diary, "Every part of the building was crowded, every aisle filled. Estimated number, two to three thousand at each meeting. There was great attention and silence, and the addresses were intensely interesting." Years later, Rev. Robert Wallcutt, an associate of William Lloyd Garrison, still remembered "the four galleries rising above the auditorium all crowded with a silent audience, carried away with the calm, simple eloquence which narrated what [Angelina] and her sister had seen from their earliest days."

Gradually a few close friends learned of Angelina's and Theodore's impending marriage. Given their importance to the abolitionist movement, such news was bound to have great impact. "We have uncommon *notoriety*," Theodore wrote to Angelina, "YOU *especially*. At this moment probably no female in the country is so extensively known . . . as *you*." In a letter to Theodore on April 7, Angelina related that when Anne Weston found out about them, she said that Weld had "risen 50 percent in her estimation," and that she considered Angelina's engagement "a complete triumph over the pastoral brethren who threatened *such women* with the entire withdrawal of

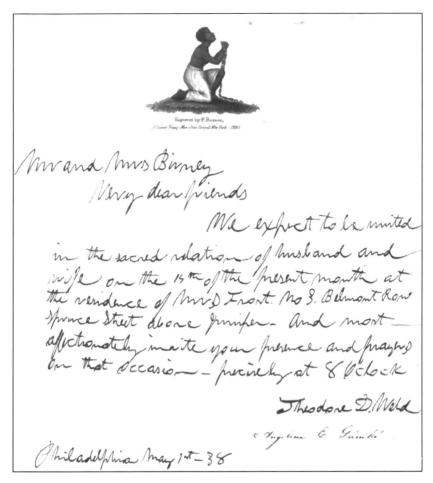

Although this wedding invitation to James and Agatha Birney is in Theodore . Weld's "scratchifications," it is signed by Angelina as well—an expression of the equality in their relationship. The Grimké-Weld wedding was to be a virtual lexicon of famous abolitionists, both black and white. *Courtesy of the Clements Library, University of Michigan*

man's protection." Angelina wrote that her abolitionist friends in Philadelphia, however, were "almost *offended* that I should do such a thing as to get married. Some say we were both public property and had *no right* to enter into such an engagement. Others that I will now be good for nothing henceforth and forever to the cause. . . ." Weld's friends also responded in various ways to the news. Some literally cried for joy; others implied that Angelina was lucky to get *any* man to marry her.*

Letters flew back and forth between Boston and New York as Angelina and Theodore made wedding preparations and decisions about their future. They decided to marry in Philadelphia, a few days before the Female Anti-Slavery Society's annual convention opened there in mid-May. Many friends would already be in the city and would not need to travel for the ceremony. Theodore emphatically stated how pleased he was to refute the property laws of the time, which gave all the wife's property to the husband as soon as they married; "a vandal law," he called it.

They decided to live in Fort Lee, New Jersey, after the wedding. There Theodore found a small house with enough land for a garden; it was close enough to commute to New York, but affordable enough for their small income. Theodore would continue to work for the American Anti-Slavery Society in the New York office. Angelina and Sarah would set up house and continue to work for the antislavery cause in some capacity, yet to be determined.

From the first, Angelina expressed unorthodox views of weddings. She didn't believe that a minister was essential to sanction the union between Theodore and herself; it was obvious that God approved, and what more was necessary? As Angelina was a Quaker and Theodore a Presbyterian, it might have been impossible to find a minister willing to perform the service anyway. The Quakers did not allow their members to marry anyone but Quakers. By marrying Weld, Angelina faced certain expulsion from the Quaker faith (and

---

*One twentieth-century historian implied that Weld married Angelina in order to keep her from speaking in public again!

Sarah faced expulsion just for attending the wedding). Sarah wrote to a lawyer in Philadelphia regarding Pennsylvania law concerning marriage. She found that it was legal to marry without ministers of any faith, if one married in the presence of witnesses and a justice of the peace. It also would be a good idea, the lawyer added, to have a contract signed by both of them.

They intended their wedding to be an interracial affair, an extraordinary event for the time. Angelina wanted to marry at her sister Anna's house in Philadelphia, but worried that Anna would not permit blacks at the wedding. Angelina wrote to Theodore that Anna had finally agreed, "from a principle of *duty*, but has no pleasure in it. Her aristocratic feelings I can plainly see are galled at the very anticipation of such a motley assembly of white and black, high and low, as we expect to have there." They planned to have a black baker make the wedding cake, using free sugar, of course, as the only sweetener. The wedding date was set for May 14, and over eighty invitations were sent out.

Theodore's brother Lewis attended, but his brothers Charles and Ezra did not. His parents and sister, who lived in Manlius, New York, were unwell and unable to come. Polly Grimké couldn't attend either, but wrote, "I feel assured that my dear daughter will marry no one who is not equal to her in every sense of the word; and from the description of your lover given by Sarah and yourself, he seems to be suitable to you in all respects. . . . May every blessing attend you both. . . ."

The last Odeon lecture took place on April 19. Angelina recounted to Theodore, "I took leave of my audience in trembling tones, committing into their hands the cause of the slave with tears." A few days later, Angelina and Sarah reunited with Weld in New York. They visited the house in Fort Lee, New

Jersey, where they would live. Then Angelina and Sarah went on to Philadelphia, while Weld remained in New York for the American Anti-Slavery Convention.

On Monday, May 14, abolitionists from across the country gathered in Philadelphia to dedicate the newly built Pennsylvania Hall. That evening, between thirty and forty guests congregated at 3 Belmont Row, Spruce Street, to witness the wedding of Angelina Emily Grimké and Theodore Dwight Weld, the "most mobbed man" and the "most notorious woman" in America.

The list of witnesses to the wedding reads like a "who's who" of signatures from the abolitionist movement. William Lloyd Garrison was there, as mild and polite in person as he was venomous in his newspaper. The poet John Greenleaf Whittier was there, but, being a Quaker, he waited outside while the wedding vows were said. Angelina's Philadelphia friends Jane Smith and Sarah and Grace Douglass were there. The Tappans, Gerrit and Anne Smith, and Henry Stanton were among the abolitionist friends of Weld who attended. From Massachusetts came the Philbricks, the Chapmans, the Westons, and Abby Kelley, who would take up public speaking for the abolition of slavery where Angelina left off. Angelina also invited Betsy Dawson and her daughter, former Grimké family slaves who lived in Philadelphia after having been freed by Angelina's sister Anna. "We thus had an opportunity," Sarah explained, "to bear our testament against the horrible prejudice which prevails against colored persons, and equally awful prejudice against the poor."

We have no account by either Angelina or Theodore of their wedding. Sarah, however, described the event to Elizabeth Pease, a friend in England:

Neither Theodore nor Angelina felt as if they could bind themselves to any preconceived form of words, and accordingly uttered such as the Lord gave them at the moment. Theodore addressed Angelina in a solemn and tender manner. He alluded to the unrighteous power vested in a husband by the laws of the United States over the person and property of his wife, and he abjured all authority, all government, save the influence which love would give to them over each other as moral and immortal beings. . . . Angelina's address to him was brief but comprehensive, containing a promise to honor him, to prefer him above herself, to love him with a pure heart fervently.

After prayers by Theodore and Angelina, a black minister, a white minister, and Sarah, "the certificate was then read by William Lloyd Garrison and signed by the company. The evening was spent in pleasant social intercourse. . . . "

Two days later, on May 16, 1838, Angelina's words rang out over the mob in the brand new Pennsylvania Hall. The following day Pennsylvania Hall was burned to the ground by anti-abolitionist rioters. Angelina didn't know it at the time, but that speech was the last time her voice would be heard in public for many years.

# ❦9❧

# . . . AND MARRIAGE

Angelina Grimké had married. She did not speak in public again for many years. Was there some connection?

Before Angelina and Theodore married, the question of her career as a public speaker arose numerous times in their correspondence. In the months between their betrothal and marriage, Angelina had begun to wonder if she were able to continue speaking in public. When she addressed the audience at the Odeon, just as at the Massachusetts state legislature, Angelina's legs trembled so much that she could barely stand. Of her first Odeon lecture, she wrote to Theodore,

> I thought yesterday perhaps our marriage was to be my dismission from *public* service. O! how I should rejoice at it, if the Master [God] should say, "*It is enough.*" It is an encreasing [sic] trial to me and most gladly would I retire from public view and sink down into *sweet obscurity*.

For Angelina, the thrill and validation of speaking in public had worn thin. Fifteen months of never laying her head on her own pillow, in her own room; of speaking out, regardless of the jeers and heckles that met her—had brought her to this threshold.

Polly Grimké echoed this wish when she acknowledged her daughter's impending marriage. "[A]fter you become a Matron,"

Polly wrote to Angelina, "I hope that you feel that retirement is best suited to your station; and you will desire to retire from the busy scenes of publicity. . . ."

Theodore may have unwittingly reinforced this idea when he suggested that their marriage would be an experiment of sorts. Could Angelina, accustomed to being in the public eye, cope with the duties of marriage? (Many people thought that abolitionist women such as Angelina would fail at the rigors of a "normal" woman's life.) And would Weld himself, who had maintained for so long the *theory* of the equality of the sexes, be able to *practice* that belief when living with his wife? Ultimately, Weld and Angelina decided to continue their public lives, and at the same time add the dimension of marriage and "taking up house" on a private level.

When Angelina married at the age of thirty-three, she had never cooked a meal, and knew nothing about housekeeping and cleaning. In some ways, she was as unlike a typical nineteenth-century woman as anyone could be. But she wanted to make up for these perceived deficiencies. After the Welds and Sarah left Philadelphia in May 1838, they visited Theodore's parents in Manlius, New York, for several weeks. Weld's mother taught Angelina and Sarah the basics of cooking and cleaning. Then the threesome returned to Fort Lee, New Jersey, to begin their new life together.

The house in Fort Lee was small but charming. It was situated on the cliffs, or palisades, overlooking the Hudson River, across which sprawled New York City. An early commuter, Theodore went into the city to work at the national office of the American Anti-Slavery Society on Nassau Street. There he supervised all of the society's publications, including its newspaper, and was involved in strategic decision-making as well.

Weld was often a passenger on the *Echo,* the ferry that crossed the Hudson daily. When Angelina heard the ferry's engine chugging upriver in the evening, she would go outside and blow a whistle. If Theodore was on board, he responded with a companion whistle, and Angelina hastened to the dock to meet her husband.

In the evenings, the three of them took moonlit walks on the cliffs. On weekends, they hiked and picnicked on the palisades. Angelina confided to Jane Smith, "[L]anguage cannot express the joy in that woman's heart who finds after she has given her heart to a man, and links her earthly destinies indissolubly with his, that he is *all* she expected, and more than she had dared to hope. . . ."

Sarah and Angelina hired a local cabinetmaker to make furniture for them of the simplest kind. Weld had window-shopped for furniture in New York City that spring, but found it "so tricked out and covered with curved work or bedizened and *gew gawed* and gilded," that he gave up in disgust. To save money, the sisters chose cherry wood over mahogany or teak.

Long before the marriage, they had decided to do without servants. Angelina was excited at the prospect of doing everything for herself. In addition, knowing that Weld was not wealthy, Angelina did not want to incur unnecessary expenses. Too, all three of them longed to live a simple life, and a simple life was one without servants. In August, barely three months after the wedding, Angelina wrote to Lydia Child, "I was utterly ashamed to let any stranger see how ignorant I was of every part of housekeeping, and therefore determined to *learn, learn*, before I undertook to direct others. And so pleased are we with our threefold cord of peerless harmony and love, that nothing but necessity will induce us to employ a domestic."

Eating was an experience in the Weld-Grimké household. All three of them adhered to the unusual, health-conscious diet prescribed by the nutritionist Sylvester Graham, who is known today as the inventor of the graham cracker. The Graham diet forbade such items as butter, tea and coffee, meat and fish, and spices like pepper. The sisters learned to make their own bread of coarsely ground whole-wheat kernels. Weld planted a garden, the produce of which supplemented their diet. Once, when two friends from New York arrived unexpectedly, they were served a typical meal of rice and molasses. But, Sarah wrote in a letter to a friend, the hosts also brought out "bread and milk, pie without shortening, and hominy," to fill the stomachs of their guests.

The sisters alternated the cooking chores weekly. Amused references to Angelina's burned food sprinkle both sisters' letters during this period. To her friend Jane, Angelina wrote, "As to how I have made out with cooking, it so happens that labor (planting a garden) gives Theodore such an appetite that everything is sweet to him, so that my rice and asparagus, potatoes, mush, and Indian bread all taste well, though some might think them not fit to eat." Sarah took to cooking enough food at one time to last an entire week, and most meals were eaten cold.

Angelina and Sarah chose to spend as little time as possible on the routines of household work (such as cooking) in order to continue devoting themselves to the abolition movement. Even though they were not speaking in public, they found much to do. Weld was working on a new book, with a goal to show slavery for what it was; the book would be made up of testimony of people who had personally witnessed slavery. Weld wrote to abolitionists near and far, calling for entries for this book, yet he received fewer replies than expected and needed.

He discovered, however, that the New York Commercial

Reading Room, a library of sorts, subscribed to various Southern newspapers, and periodically cleaned the shelves of old editions, which were sold for waste. Weld bought discarded newspapers from the years 1837 to 1839, from cities such as Charleston, New Orleans, Vicksburg, Raleigh, and Mobile. He brought the papers home, where Angelina and Sarah sorted through them. They then chose passages that used Southerners' own words to condemn slavery.

The sisters spent six months gathering information for Theodore's book. After they were done, they went up to the attic of the Fort Lee house to see how many sources they had used. They stopped counting at 20,000. In the table of contents of the completed book, Weld detailed witnesses' personal narratives about slavery; topics such as "Clothing," "Punishments," "Food," "Slave Breeding," and "Cruelty to Women Slaves" are common in the testimonies.

The result was one of the most powerful antislavery books ever printed. *American Slavery as It Is: Testimony of a Thousand Witnesses* was published in 1839. Historian Dwight Dumond called it "the most crushing indictment of any institution ever written." It was over 200 pages long and sold for 37 ½ cents a copy. By the end of the first year of publication, over 100,000 copies had been sold. All profits went to the American Anti-Slavery Society. The book was published anonymously, a testament to Weld's utter lack of egotism.

Until the publication of *Uncle Tom's Cabin* thirteen years later, *American Slavery as It Is* was the most widely read work of abolition literature. In fact, it provided Harriet Beecher Stowe with much of the information regarding slavery that she used in *Uncle Tom's Cabin*. Apparently, Mrs. Stowe even slept with *American Slavery as It Is* under her pillow when she was writing her book.

Not only did Sarah and Angelina do much of the research for the book, but Angelina also recopied Theodore's entire manuscript by hand, of course, to make it legible for the publisher. For both Sarah and Angelina, the most difficult task of all was supplying their extensive personal testimony of the horrors of slavery for the book. Following are just a few excerpts from Angelina's account of slavery as she knew it in Charleston:

> I remember very well that when I was a child, our next door neighbor whipped a young woman so brutally, that in order to escape his blows she rushed through the drawing-room window in the second story, and fell upon the street pavement below and broke her hip. This circumstance produced no excitement or inquiry.
>
> The following circumstance occurred in Charleston, in 1828:
>
> A slaveholder, after flogging a little girl about thirteen years old, set her on a table with her feet fastened in a pair of stocks. He then locked the door and took out the key. When the door was opened she was found dead, having fallen from the table. When I asked a prominent lawyer, who belonged to one of the first families in the State, whether the murderer of this helpless child could not be indicted, he coolly replied, that the slave was Mr. _____'s property, and if he chose to suffer the *loss,* no one else had any thing to do with it. The loss of *human life*, the distress of the parents and other relatives of the little girl, seemed utterly out of his thoughts: it was the loss of *property* only that presented itself to his mind.

Recalling and describing the scenes each had witnessed took its toll on both sisters. While neither used the names of the slaveholders whose stories they told, their family members in Charleston could easily see themselves and their acquaintances in these eyewitness accounts. Once again, the sisters distressed

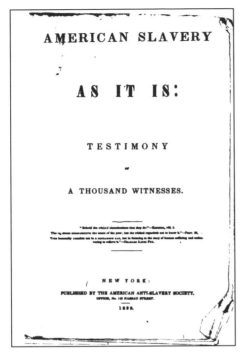

No author is listed on the title page of *American Slavery as It Is,* a testament to Theodore Weld's humility. Weld received no royalties or other payment for this or any of his writings. The profits went directly to the American Anti-Slavery Society. From Dumond, *Antislavery Origins of the Civil War in the United States*

their relatives and brought shame upon the Grimké family name.

Their sister Eliza wrote to imply that the only positive outcome of *American Slavery as It Is* was that their mother, Polly, was spared its publication. Polly had taken ill in mid-July and died in her sleep on July 21, 1839. She was seventy-five years old. Since her marriage the previous year, Angelina had grown closer to her mother than ever before; letters practically flew between the two of them during the first half of 1839. Angelina and Sarah were heartbroken at their mother's death, not only for the sheer loss of her, but because despite their efforts, she died a slaveholder and would carry that sin to her grave. Still, in a letter to a friend, Angelina characterized Polly as "the promoter of every benevolent enterprize [sic] in Charleston. . . ."

Polly had promised to leave her slaves to Sarah and Angelina upon her death, and she kept her word. She owned only four slaves by this time, having pared down her belongings as she grew older. The sisters immediately arranged for the two slaves and their two children to be freed. They also offered to help care for a former house slave, Stephen, who had health problems and could not earn his keep; and Stephen eventually came to live with them.

After Polly's death, Angelina wrote to her sister Anna in Philadelphia, who shared the other siblings' disapproval of Sarah and Angelina's actions. Angelina tried to justify to Anna her contribution in *American Slavery as It Is*, "What we have written we have written from a deep and solemn sense of duty, and neither life nor *death* can shake the rock of principle upon which we stand. It cost us more *agony of soul* to write those testimonies than any thing we ever did. . . ."

Angelina's health had begun to suffer after her marriage. Abby Kelley, the abolitionist speaker, visited the Weld-Grimké household in the spring of 1839, and wrote to Anne Warren Weston about Angelina's condition.

> I went there with a determination to rebuke them [the sisters] severely for absenting themselves from the N. Y. meetings, but found to my own mortification that I had passed judgement before examining the witnesses. Angelina is truly very feeble. Their opinion is, that her labors in lecturing were altogether too great for a constitution naturally very slender and that she will never recover from it. Shock. Then last winter she applied herself too closely in assisting to get out "Slavery as it is," which has entirely prostrated her physical as well as mental energies. . . .

Abby added that Sarah felt she needed to assist Angelina and therefore was not attending meetings.

Indeed, from this period on, Angelina seemed to suffer injuries, both internal and external, that limited her activities for the remainder of her life. In a memorial to his wife after her death years later, Theodore wrote,

> These injuries, though wholly unlike, were in their effect a unit, one causing, the other intensifying a lifelong weakness. Together they shattered incurably her nervous system. . . . Such was the effect upon her, that ever after she was forced to avoid exciting scenes and topics, especially slavery, its effects upon slave and master, also the wrongs of woman as wrought out in her legal, ecclesiastical, educational, and political disabilities. . . .

The nature of these injuries is a puzzle to Angelina's biographers. Historian Gerda Lerner suggests a medical condition such as a hernia or a prolapsed uterus, which Victorians like Theodore and Angelina never would have specified in public. These conditions were inoperable then, whereas today they are easily corrected with surgery. Another biographer, Katherine DuPre Lumpkin, concludes that Angelina was browbeaten by Theodore and Sarah into not speaking in public; but such an accusation seems groundless. It is likely that the requirements of an impoverished daily life exhausted Angelina's capacities; a medical condition would only have intensified this state.

Yet another event may have contributed to Angelina's feeling poorly after the publication of *American Slavery as It Is,* and that was her first pregnancy. We do not know much about Angelina's pregnancies, because women at that time generally did not discuss such delicate matters in letters. During their courtship, however, Angelina had confessed to Weld that she was not fond of children; the thought of approaching motherhood may have contributed some degree of anxiety to her already poor health.

Charles Stuart Faucheraud Weld was born on December 14, 1839. Judging from her letters of that period, Angelina seemed to have overcome her distaste for children. "The idea," she wrote to a friend, "of a baby exercising moral influence never came into my mind until I felt its power on my own heart. I used to think all a parent's reward for early care and anxiety was reaped in after-life, save the enjoyment of an infant as a pretty plaything. But the Lord has taught me differently. . . ." Her only sorrow was that she was unable to breastfeed her baby because of an infection.

Angelina was nearly thirty-five when little Charley was born. Like many mature mothers, she took her role seriously, faithfully studying parenting manuals in the months before Charley's birth. *Physiological and Moral Management of Infancy* by Andrew Combe instructed mothers to feed babies one tablespoonful at a time, *just five times daily*. Angelina conscientiously carried out these directions, not understanding why Charley fretted so. One day, however, when she and Theodore were away, Sarah took over the feedings and decided to let Charley drink as much as he wanted. The results were amazing. The Welds returned to find the baby satisfied for once, and after that common sense took the place of Combe's manual.

When the Grimké sisters stopped speaking in public, the cracks in the abolition movement did not miraculously heal. Instead, they grew worse. First, in 1839, the antislavery movement in Massachusetts split into two groups. At issue was not only the woman question, but whether the movement should maintain its primary focus on slavery, or take on a score of other reform causes as well. The Garrisonians, many of whom were friends of Sarah and Angelina, preferred to tackle a wide range of reforms. Weld and the sisters, on the other hand, believed that if slavery became one of many concerns, then the end goal of freeing the slaves would never be accomplished.

Many of Garrison's opponents within the antislavery movement felt that there was no room for discussion or dissension once Garrison had spoken. The Reverend Amos Phelps despised the subservience of Garrison's followers and insisted that he too could work for freedom "without doing it through your [Garrison's] paper, and without coming and kneeling devoutly to ask your Holiness whether I may do so or not." Henry B. Stanton reported that "the split is wide, and can never be closed up. . . ."

The following year, 1840, the split spread to the national antislavery movement. Garrison "packed" the national convention in New York City by hiring a boat to bring his followers down from Massachusetts. The Garrisonian majority appointed a woman, Abby Kelley, to the business committee of the American Anti-Slavery Society. The conservative minority, many of whom were Weld's friends and co-workers, walked out of the convention and formed a new group, the American and Foreign Anti-Slavery Society. This group was not open to women. Some members of this group turned to political action instead of moral persuasion; in 1840 and 1844, for example, James G. Birney ran for president on the Liberty Party ticket.

The Welds and Sarah chose to distance themselves from both groups. They did not believe in Garrison's ideas but could not support a group that was closed to women. Weld had lost faith in reform groups in general, seeing them as means of aggrandizing their own leaders. "What mere mechanism and artificiality!" he wrote to Angelina in 1846. "What mouthings, posturings, 'Mr. Presidents' . . . . Father forgive them—they know not what they do. And Oh may we whose eyes thou [God] hast opened to see these shadows and fictions, be vitally possessed of those *realities* which are life." More patient, Angelina wrote to Sarah Douglass, "We mourn that there are divisions amongst us, that abolitionists have their Pauls and their Apollos' but we rejoice that Jehovah reigns, that the cause of the slave is his cause, and that although this falling out by the way may retard, it cannot prevent the triumph of truth."

Some friendships declined over the Weld-Grimkés' reluctance to be involved in what they saw as a squabble. In 1842 Garrison questioned in *The Liberator*, "Where is Theodore D. Weld and his wife, and Sarah M. Grimké? All 'in the quiet,' and far removed from all strife! . . . Once the land was shaken by their free spirits, but now they are neither seen nor felt."

The split in the antislavery movement further weakened the finances of the national organization, which had already been crippled by the Panic of 1837 and its aftermath. The Panic of 1837 was the nation's first major depression. Many businesses went bankrupt, banks ran out of money and closed, and unemployed workers demonstrated in the streets. The philanthropists who aided the national antislavery organization were themselves severely hurt by the panic. Rather than flourishing, the organization withered, and Theodore voluntarily cut his salary at this time, so as to preserve what little resources the organization had.

This economic downturn affected the Welds in another way. Angelina had invested her paternal inheritance (a sum of about $5,000, which would be equivalent to $73,500 today) with the Philadelphia Quaker Isaac Lloyd. The Welds requested the money, and Lloyd promised to send it, but it never materialized. Lloyd was one more victim of the Panic of 1837, and he passed his loss of funds on to the Welds. Angelina and

Theodore had counted on this inheritance to keep them afloat. In a letter to Lewis Tappan in 1840, Theodore asked to borrow money when Isaac Lloyd's promises turned out to be empty. "I dont [sic] see but we must *stop eating*," he exclaimed.

Theodore had always wanted to own a farm, and the three-some decided that by purchasing and running a farm, they could be more self-sufficient. They found a 62-acre farm in Belleville, New Jersey, a few miles north of Newark. It was situated on a rise along the Passaic River, and had beautiful grounds and views. The farm had once belonged to Revolutionary War General Nathanael Greene.

The large stone and clapboard house was originally built in the 1700s. Two magnificent willows stood in front of the house. A long line of spruce and hemlock trees stretched to the south. Maple and walnut trees, lilacs and rosebushes, adorned the grounds as well, giving the farm an air of grace and seclusion.

The fifteen-room house permitted the Welds and Sarah to act on their hospitable impulses to a much greater extent than in Fort Lee. A steady stream of friends and relatives visited the farm in Belleville, further straining the family's resources. Sister Anna and her daughter Marianna spent the summer. Polly's ex-slave Stephen came to live with them. Weld's parents and siblings ended up living with them until their deaths. Angelina's childhood friend Elizabeth Bascom was in poor financial straits and spent a year at Belleville. And their Quaker and abolitionist friends came and stayed too—Sarah Douglass, Jane Smith, Abby Kelley, to name but a few.

In 1840, Henry B. Stanton came to visit with his new bride, Elizabeth Cady Stanton. She had heard a great deal about the sisters and eagerly anticipated meeting them. To her disappointment, when she and Henry arrived the house looked bare, "severely destitute of all tasteful, womanly touches." The food

The World Anti-Slavery Convention in London in 1840 was one in a series of events that tore the antislavery movement apart. But new movements were being born. Refused seats by their British hosts, Elizabeth Cady Stanton and American delegate Lucretia Mott sat in the gallery and vowed to hold a convention for women's rights. *Courtesy of the Library of Congress, LC-USZ62-15060*

was cold and very simple—not the tea and hot beefsteak that Elizabeth expected. "But," she recalled, "the chilling environments of these noble people were modified by the sincere hospitality with which we were received. . . . How changed was the atmosphere of that home to me the next day." By the time the Stantons left, Elizabeth was on intimate terms with both Sarah and Angelina. Shortly after this visit, the Stantons sailed to England for the World Anti-Slavery Convention. In a letter to the Weld-Grimkés from London, Elizabeth wrote, "Dear friends, how much I love you!! What a trio! for me to love. You have no idea what a hold you have on my heart."

Elizabeth Cady Stanton attended the World Anti-Slavery Convention as a spectator. But some American women came as delegates, only to find on their arrival that the British Anti-Slavery Society, host of the convention, refused to seat them.

Lucretia Mott was such a woman. While seated in the gallery together, Mott and Stanton vowed to hold a convention for American women. Eight years later, under their direction, the first woman's rights convention in history would be held in Seneca Falls, New York.

The birth of Theodore Grimké Weld on January 3, 1841, welcomed the new year in Belleville. After this birth, Angelina hired domestic help and found mothering an infant easier than the first time. Sarah adored the boys wholeheartedly, as if they were her own. And so the family began to settle down to farm life. But before they became too comfortable, their lives would change again, with Angelina and Sarah discovering, first-hand, how hard an ordinary woman's life could be.

# ❧10❧

# AND THE
# WAR CAME

In the 1830s abolitionists used moral suasion (that is, persuasion) to convince Americans that slavery must be destroyed. In the 1840s they turned to another means—politics. Some abolitionists ran for Congress, with the intent of changing the laws from within. Their timing was perfect, for in 1841 the gag rule, which prevented petitions about slavery from being introduced on the floor of the House of Representatives, had been voted a *permanent* rule of procedure. By letting that rule stand, Congress was agreeing that slavery was a forbidden topic. And if it couldn't be discussed, how could it be changed?

In Congress, the handful of antislavery Whigs—a major political party at that time—resolved to fight this rule. Among them were Joshua Leavitt, former Executive Committee member of the American Anti-Slavery Society, and Joshua Giddings, Seth Gates, and Sherlock Andrews, all converted to abolitionism by Theodore Weld in the 1830s. Now Leavitt asked Weld to come to Washington and help them do the necessary research to present strong arguments on the House floor. Weld wrote to Lewis Tappan, "[T]hose men [in Congress] are in a position to do for the A.S. [antislavery] cause by a single speech more than our best lecturers can do in a year. . . . I dare not assume the responsibility of refusing

121

to comply with such a request." Even though the trip meant that he had to borrow money from Tappan to hire help on the farm that winter, Angelina insisted that he go. With her and Sarah's blessings, Theodore arrived in Washington on December 30, 1841.

And so, Sarah and Angelina ran the farm by themselves that winter, in addition to caring for one-year-old Theodore, nicknamed "Thoda," and two-year-old Charley. There were animals to feed, wood to chop and fires to make, fences to fix. They used a sleigh to go to town for shopping, traveling miles on snowy or icy roads. Angelina's letters to Theodore at this time reflect all the concerns of the farm, household, and children; they reflect how much she missed him, yet how proud she was of his contribution to the cause.

Leading the battle against the gag rule in the House of Representatives was "Old Man Eloquent," ex-president John Quincy Adams, now seventy-five years old. Early in 1842, the Southern congressmen moved to censure Adams for his presentation of a petition to dissolve the Union because of its attachment to slavery; this tactic hid the Southerners' true motive, which was to silence Adams from continuing to read petitions on the floor of Congress, despite the gag rule. Censure is a form of punishment by fellow congressmen, expressing disapproval of a congressman's behavior. Censuring an ex-president would be a serious and historic step. Weld aided Adams with research in his defense, such as locating documents that would support the right of congressmen to argue the legality of slavery, and they discussed strategies together.* Adams defended himself

---

*At this time Adams also revealed to Weld that the Grimké sisters were actually cousins of his mother, Abigail Adams, the strongest feminist of the Revolutionary era.

for a week on the House floor, ultimately forcing the House to table the censure motion forever. Weld wrote to Angelina, "The triumph of Mr. Adams is complete. This is the first victory over the slaveholders in a body ever yet achieved since the foundation of the government, and from this time their downfall takes its date." Two years later, in 1844, the gag rule, too, would be voted down by the House of Representatives.

Theodore returned home in April, and began madly attending to the many needs of the farm. He planted hundreds of fruit trees, plowed the ground for the vegetable crop, and fixed fences. He had originally thought the farm would consume three or four hours a day of his time; instead he found it was taking eleven or twelve hours. Angelina and Sarah helped as they could, but Angelina's health was not strong. When Weld left for Washington again in December 1842, Angelina was expecting their third child. This time her feelings about the separation were more polarized. "Beloved, I miss you more than I can express. I can't think of you or talk of you without my heart and eye filling." In February 1843, Angelina suffered a miscarriage. Weld returned home as soon as he could, and once again devoted himself to the seemingly endless work at the farm.

In her weakened state, Angelina did not have the strength to care for the two boys. It was fortunate that Sarah was there to help with the children, just as, almost forty years earlier, she had mothered the baby Angelina. The boys called her "Aunt Sai," and her affection for them was like a mother's.

Angelina became pregnant again just months after the miscarriage. On March 22, 1844, she delivered a healthy baby girl, Sarah Grimké Weld. Her physical health improved, but Angelina was sunk in depression. She was thirty-nine years old. The care of the children, the financial worries of the farm, Theodore's endless toil—this did not fulfill the expectations she had had for her life when she married six years earlier.

Over the years, Angelina had espoused a variety of Protestant faiths—first she was an Episcopalian, then a Presbyterian, and finally, a Quaker. Following her marriage, both she and Sarah abandoned organized religions, though maintaining their faith in God and Christ. And yet, in the early 1840s, Angelina turned for comfort to a utopian religion, Millerism. An outgrowth of the revivalism of the Second Great Awakening, Millerism prophesied that the kingdom of God was near at hand. Its founder, William Miller, believed that Christ's advent would take place sometime between March 21, 1843, and March 21, 1844.

At its height, Millerism attracted at least 50,000 fervent followers and perhaps a million more who thought it plausible. Like many others, Angelina sought respite in the promise of an otherworldly delivery from present problems and disappointments. However, when March 21, 1844 (the day before baby Sarah's birth), came and went with no great revelation, people grew skeptical of Millerism. A second date, in October 1844, was predicted; that, too, passed uneventfully. Theodore had always scoffed at Millerism; now, Angelina, too, was forced to acknowledge the falseness of the faith. It was a low point in her life.

Theodore now was forty-one years old. His work for the American Anti-Slavery Society dwindled after the split in the movement. He, too, must have felt he was wasting his time as a manual laborer. Angelina recognized this and felt for him. "[T]he fear often comes over me like a dark cloud, that we are not doing the will of God," she wrote to Theodore in 1849. "We are not fulfilling our destiny and yet I cannot see anything definite—don't see any particular thing, to do." She continued, "It seems to me dearest One . . . the time must have come for you to give up your drudging. You greatly *mistake me* if you think it pleases me to see *you* working as you do on the farm—in such a state of mind—because you feel constantly that you are *not* in your right place. . . ."

Gradually Angelina and Theodore identified a way of life that suited them. As their children grew older, they began spending several hours a day educating them. Then, beginning in 1848, they took in several boarder-students as well. Before long, nearly twenty students attended the Welds' Belleville School. Among them were the children of many of their reformer friends, including the sons of Gerrit and Anne Smith, Henry and Elizabeth Cady Stanton, and James Birney, and Elizur Wright's daughter, Ellie. From Charleston came their nephew Thomas, son of Angelina's brother Henry.

The school thrived, with Theodore as the principal. Instruction was offered in composition, history, French, mathematics, and drawing. Angelina taught history, her favorite subject. That Angelina loved teaching (beyond the preschool level) is not surprising, since many years earlier she had considered it as a profession. Sarah reluctantly taught French, not confident of her grasp of the language nor comfortable in the role of authoritarian. Theodore placed great emphasis on the moral development of the students, in addition to academic progress. Angelina and Sarah did all the cooking, cleaning, and caring for the students. And so began a new era in Angelina's life.

That same year, Lucretia Mott and Elizabeth Cady Stanton made good on their pledge of eight years earlier to hold a convention on woman's rights. The woman's rights movement for-

Elizabeth Cady Stanton

# From Abolition to Woman's Rights

The Grimké sisters were not the first women to join the abolition movement, but they were the first to reveal and rebel against the limited sphere that most men of the day expected women to operate within. At that time, to think of woman as man's equal was absurd. Angelina and Sarah broke down the barriers that prevented women from speaking in public. From there, it was not a long jump to woman suffrage, married women's rights, child welfare reform, and equal educational and job opportunities.

The Grimké sisters acted as a vanguard for other women leaders. Before Angelina spoke in public, Lucretia Mott's speaking was limited to Quaker meetinghouses. When Angelina addressed the Massachusetts legislative committee, Mott wrote to a friend that the Grimké sisters were doing a noble part in correcting "the low estimate of woman's labors." Both Elizabeth Cady Stanton and Lucy Stone were younger than Angelina and regarded her as a mentor, as they carried on the struggle for woman's rights through the nineteenth century.

mally began on July 19, 1848, in Seneca Falls, New York, where Stanton had recently moved with her family. Neither Sarah nor Angelina participated in that historic event, but Angelina made her interest in the movement known. She began to emerge from her self-imposed exile from reform movements. In 1850 she was elected to the Central Committee of the Woman's Rights Convention held in Worcester, Massachusetts, but she was unable to attend. She did attend the convention in 1851 in Rochester, New York. The following year both she and Sarah contributed letters of support and encouragement to the convention in Syracuse, New York.

Running the Belleville School and keeping up repairs on the farm took most of the Welds' financial and physical resources. It was a hard life. In addition, Angelina was unhappy with the limitations of their children's education. She wrote, "Although home education has some advantages, yet I am satisfied that it never can expand the hearts of our children as we want to see them expand, and as they must be expanded in order that they may be useful in developing the great principles of Love practically in their generation." In 1853 a new opportunity was offered to them, which seemed to solve many of their problems.

The Welds and Sarah were invited to join the Raritan Bay Union (RBU), a new cooperative community of between thirty and forty families who held similar views on religion and education. The members of the cooperative bought a 270-acre property on the Raritan Bay, near Perth Amboy, New Jersey; each member contributed a $1,000 investment in the venture. Families had separate living apartments, but shared eating

Opposite: Elizabeth Cady Stanton with her daughter Harriot in 1856. *Courtesy of the Stanton Family Collection*

and common areas. They shared the cooking and cleaning chores too.

The RBU planned to open a school, Eagleswood, and they invited Weld to be the principal and to teach, with Angelina and Sarah teaching classes too. Such a move would be a great opportunity for Theodore. Angelina could see that it would also lighten their loads considerably—no farm to worry about, and far fewer housekeeping chores for Angelina and Sarah. It would also satisfy Angelina's desire for a more expansive education for the children, now aged fourteen, twelve, and nine.

Angelina and Theodore were eager to participate. Sarah, however, did not think that a cooperative community would be a positive setting for her. Added to this difference of opinion between Angelina and Sarah was a financial matter: Sarah had been lending money to the Welds, which, Angelina told her sister Mary, "has long been *painfully heavy on my heart.*" With the sale of Belleville, Angelina hoped to repay the debt to Sarah.

Yet another breach between the sisters developed as a result of Angelina's illnesses, which often incapacitated her. When bedridden, Angelina had depended on and been grateful for Sarah's help. Sarah, too, found personal fulfillment in her role as Aunt Sai. To Sarah Douglass she wrote, "In our precious children my desolate heart found a sweet response to its love. They have saved me from I know not what of horrible despair. . . ." But Sarah's gift of love and care was a double-edged sword; to her dismay and anguish, Angelina found her children consistently turning to Sarah rather than to her, just as she had turned to Sarah forty years earlier. Once she realized what was happening and why, Angelina tried to change the pattern, to right the balance within the family. She and Sarah eventually took turns minding the children, so that they would learn to turn to their mother with their needs.

In early 1854, while Sarah was away on a visit, Angelina wrote to her, finally able to express her concerns over the past fifteen years of living together:

> There are times dear Sister when I feel humbled in the dust, because I never have been willing to share my blessings with you *equally*—Often, very often, when I look at all the sorrows and disappointments you have met with in life and all that you have done for me, I feel ashamed and confounded at my ingratitude and self-ishness. Then again it seems unnatural that a wife and a Mother should ever thus be willing equally to share of the affections of her dearest ones with any human being. . . . I often feel weary of a conflict which has lasted 15 years and wonder when and what will be the end of it.

Offended, Sarah offered to move out, but was taken aback when Angelina agreed that it would be a good idea, at least for a while.

For the first time in almost twenty years, the sisters lived separately. Sarah lived apart from the family for almost all of 1854. She stayed for a while with Anne and Gerrit Smith in up-state New York, then in Boston with her friend Dr. Harriet Hunt, a noted woman's rights activist and physician. At first Sarah thought of doing legal research on the status of women. She traveled to Washington to do the necessary research, which led her to consider studying medicine. But Sarah was over sixty years old then, and it was just too hard, particularly at that time, for a woman of her age to begin the process of break-ing into a profession. Ultimately Angelina invited Sarah to move back with the family at Eagleswood—"We all want you with us," Angelina wrote her—and Sarah accepted. This argument between the sisters does not appear to have arisen again; both accepted each other's shortcomings and resolved to live peaceably. In the fall of 1854 the Welds moved to Eagleswood, and by late December, Sarah had joined them there.

With the family's move to Raritan Bay Union, Angelina and Theodore established one of the finest and most innovative educational institutions in the country. Eagleswood differed from the typical school in many ways. For one, it was coeducational—not surprising, considering their beliefs about woman's rights. Also, although it was grounded in a belief in God, Eagleswood had no particular religious affiliation. In addition to the three Rs as a curriculum (common in most schools), Eagleswood offered gymnastics, science, music, art, and literature. Students not only studied Shakespeare, but performed the plays as well.

When Eagleswood opened its doors in 1854, fifty-six boarders were enrolled, in addition to children of the RBU community. Within several years the RBU had folded, but the school continued and became renowned, particularly among reform-minded families.

Weld believed in developing all aspects of the child—moral, physical, intellectual, and aesthetic. Unlike most schools of the day, teachers at Eagleswood encouraged students to ask questions. Angelina taught arithmetic and writing; Weld taught grammar, composition, and literature; and Sarah taught French and kept the account books. Several other teachers handled the rest of the curriculum. Adults and students met in the parlor for dancing on Saturday nights. On Sundays, after a religious service, people met in the parlor to discuss current issues.

Eagleswood and the Raritan Bay Union were founded by Marcus and Rebecca Spring, New England Quakers and prominent abolitionists. Theodore Weld established an unusual and innovative curriculum at the Eagleswood School (the large building at right) to develop all aspects of the child student. From Meltzer and Harding, *A Thoreau Profile*

Eagleswood became a cultural mecca for liberal thinkers. Visitors included the poet and newspaper editor William Cullen Bryant; Horace Greeley (founder of *The New York Herald*, and instrumental in pushing the idea of westward expansion); and Henry David Thoreau (author of *Walden, or Life in the Woods* and the essay "Civil Disobedience").

In their strolls to the nearby town of Perth Amboy, Angelina and Sarah managed to shock the local people by wearing "bloomers," a costume which consisted of a skirt or dress reaching to the knee or below, under which were loose pantaloons, fastened at the ankle. In an age where women wore long skirts, bloomers were considered shocking because they showed a woman's legs. Bloomers became a symbol of woman's rights activists, since they proclaimed the right of women to dress for comfort and practicality.

National events intruded upon life at Eagleswood as they had not at Belleville. Perhaps this was due in part to the presence of abolitionists and other activists at the school. But it would have been hard to hide from American politics anywhere in the late 1850s. The seeds of slavery were coming to fruition.

In 1854 Congress passed the Kansas-Nebraska Act, which opened the territories of Kansas and Nebraska to settlement, leaving the decision of whether to be a slave state or free state to the territory itself. Bloodshed and chaos ensued in Kansas over the next few years, as settlers of both persuasions tried to make their practices dominant. Both the North and the South rallied to the polarized factions in Kansas. At Eagleswood, twelve-year-old Sarah Weld, along with her classmates, collected donations and made knick-knacks to sell for the benefit of the "free-soilers" of Kansas.

In 1859 abolitionist John Brown captured a federal arsenal in Harpers Ferry, Virginia, and tried to start a slave revolt. He and six of his accomplices left alive were caught, jailed, and sentenced to death. Hysteria reached new heights in the North and the South. To the South, John Brown was evil incarnate; to the North, he was a hero and a martyr. Eagleswood resident Rebecca Spring visited the condemned men and promised two of them that she would make sure they were buried on "free soil." Angelina, unable to bear the anxiety of the times, took to her bed for days, certain that the strife she had feared for so long was imminent. After the hangings, Rebecca Spring brought the bodies in their coffins to Eagleswood. As the boat docked on Raritan Bay, proslavery sympathizers in Perth Amboy threatened to throw the bodies overboard. But Eagleswood men and boys guarded the coffins as they were unloaded and after they were interred, and violence was narrowly averted.

As each incident in the late 1850s passed, tension and passions ran higher throughout the country. Pacifists in the past, both Angelina and Theodore became strong supporters of the Northern cause. Long before, Weld had realized that the North and South could not settle their differences without war. "Nothing short of miracles, constant miracles, and such as the world has never seen can keep at bay the two great antagonist forces. . . . *The end must come*," he wrote. And Angelina wrote to Gerrit Smith, "You see how warlike I have become—O yes—war is better than slavery."

Republican Abraham Lincoln was elected president on November 6, 1860. Within weeks, Angelina's home state of South Carolina seceded from the Union, convinced that Lincoln's first act in office would be to free the slaves. Six more states followed South Carolina's lead, forming the Confederate States of America. When Confederate forces fired on Fort Sumter in April 1861, four more Southern states joined the Confederacy. The Civil War had begun.

The sons, sons-in-law, and even grandsons of many of the Welds' old friends joined the Union Army and fought in the war. These young men were heroes to Northern society. At twenty-one, Charles Stuart Weld was a student at Harvard College when the war broke out. Instead of fighting for "the cause," Stuart (as he called himself) chose to be a conscientious objector, one who does not fight, usually because of a belief in pacifism. In Stuart's case, he just felt that the war was wrong. The Welds could not understand Stuart's position, and it pained them deeply.

Even more painful for Angelina and Theodore was the illness of their second son, Thody. Just a year before the war began, when he was eighteen, he came down with an inexplicable and incurable illness. He would sit motionless for hours, and was unable to work or study for any length of time. Perhaps today he would be diagnosed with depression, schizophrenia, chronic fatigue syndrome, or even a psychosomatic illness; it is hard to evaluate his true condition based on the letters of the past. Angelina and Theodore took Thody to specialist after specialist; eventually they placed him in an institution. It broke his loving parents' and aunt's hearts, but this appeared to be where he functioned best.

Both Theodore and Angelina contributed to the war effort in the way they knew best. In 1862 William Lloyd Garrison invited Theodore to speak in Boston, thus beginning the healing between the two antislavery campaigners. Weld's voice had healed over the years, and his speeches in Boston were so successful that he began touring New England and addressing church congregations in support of the war. He also campaigned for the Republican candidate in an election in New Hampshire. This was more of a public service than you might imagine, for the North was not solidly behind either the war or President Lincoln during those critical years. Angelina was contented to see Theodore speaking to audiences again; to Gerrit Smith, who served in Congress in the 1850s, she wrote, "He is doing the very thing my heart wants him to do."

For Angelina, too, the war brought a reawakening to political activism. Woman's rights advocates had been meeting annually since their historic gathering in 1848. Now they decided to postpone their demands until the war's end, and to throw their energies into supporting the Northern cause. They created the National Woman's Loyal League in 1863, "to give support to the government in so far as it makes a war for freedom."

Angelina's old friends and admirers had not forgotten the power of her words. On May 14, 1863, Angelina spoke in public again, nearly twenty-five years to the day since her last speech, and on the twenty-fifth anniversary of her marriage to Theodore. She addressed the National Convention of the

Woman's League. As a South Carolinian, Angelina urged the people of the North to pursue their course in the war. "Never falter, never abandon the principles which you have adopted," she declared. "God be praised. Abolitionists never sought place or power. All they asked was freedom; all they wanted was that the white man should take his foot off the negro's neck."

On the second day of the convention, Angelina presented a resolution which was adopted by the League; it was an address to the Union soldiers of the Civil War, which Angelina called "our Second Revolution." In it she pointed out that this was not a war of regional sections or of political parties, but a war of principles. "Soldiers of this revolution," she wrote, "to your hands is committed the sacred duty of carrying out . . . the ideal of our fathers, which was to secure to ALL 'life, liberty, and the pursuit of happiness,' and to every State, 'a republican form of government.'" Angelina wrote this just weeks before the Battle of Gettysburg, and six months before Lincoln wrote the Gettysburg Address, in which he, too, declared that the "great task" of the North in the Civil War was the re-establishment of democracy.

The League collected 400,000 signatures for a petition urging Congress to free all the slaves immediately. The petition evolved into the Thirteenth Amendment to the Constitution, passed by Congress in 1865.

Throughout the war Angelina and Sarah tried to continue their correspondence with their siblings in South Carolina. Their brother Henry had died in 1852, and Charles in 1857. Their oldest brother John was an invalid, and the sisters sent him support when they could until his death in 1864. Two sisters, Mary and Eliza, lived in the family home in Charleston, still defiantly defending slavery. Union forces blockaded all

The city of Charleston in 1864, taken by photographer Mathew Brady. The Civil War ended forever the graceful civilization built on the backs of slaves. *Courtesy of the Library of Congress, LC-B8171-3448*

Southern ports, including Charleston. Early in the war the blockade was relatively ineffective. As the war progressed, however, the blockade grew tighter, and Charlestonians suffered as food and other necessities grew scarce.

The Civil War brought an end to many things—hundreds of thousands of lives, a way of life in the South, and of course, finally, slavery. It also brought an end to the Eagleswood School. With the disruption caused by the war, enrollment dropped, and Eagleswood School could not sustain itself financially. In 1863 the school closed its doors. The Welds and Sarah moved to Massachusetts, there to live out the final years of their lives.

# ◀II▶

# CONFRONTING
# THE PAST

APRIL 9, 1865. General Robert E. Lee surrendered the Army of Northern Virginia to General Ulysses S. Grant. The Civil War was over.

The war's toll on the nation was staggering. More than half a million men lost their lives—260,000 from the Confederacy and 360,000 from the Union. No other war in American history has been as costly.

The South lay in ruins. Union General William Tecumseh Sherman had marched his forces through Georgia and the Carolinas, wreaking a 60-mile-wide swath of destruction as a means of hastening the war's end. He bypassed Charleston, but years of bombardment, and the fires that followed, did the job for him. In 1864, a Charleston lady described a visit to the lower part of the city, where the Grimké house stood, as "going from life to death. The streets were overgrown with grass, and formerly well-kept gardens were obliterated. . . . [T]he houses were indescribable—all of their windows were broken, many chimneys had fallen . . . piazzas were half gone, and the street looked like it was scattered with diamonds from the broken glass."

Even before the end of the war, Angelina's sisters Mary and Eliza survived on the edge of poverty. Their house was a

shell. The slaves were gone. The Grimké wealth had evapo-
rated. For months Mary and Eliza lived on water and hominy,
a kind of hulled corn. As soon as the war ended, Sarah and
Angelina sent them several hundred dollars' worth of supplies, and begged them to join them up North, even though
Mary and Eliza maintained their belief in "slavery and the
Confederacy."

With the children grown and no longer living at home,
Angelina, Theodore, and Sarah had resettled in Massachusetts
in 1863. They bought a house on Fairmount Avenue in Hyde
Park, a suburb south of Boston. Dr. Dio Lewis, a famed homeo-
pathic physician, offered them teaching positions at his boarding school for young ladies in Lexington. The Welds and Sarah
spent the weekdays in Lexington and came home on weekends,
because the twenty-mile distance between Lexington and
Hyde Park was too far to travel daily.

Mary and Eliza were preparing to come North from
Charleston to live with their sisters when Mary died unexpectedly at the age of seventy-six. Eliza, age sixty-eight, came
alone, and helped care for the Hyde Park house when the
Welds and Sarah were in Lexington. Eliza, as Sarah put it, was
"a sunbeam in the family," despite all she had been through. Yet
she must have missed home, for in 1866 she returned to
Charleston with Anna, her older sister from Philadelphia. Eliza
died in Charleston in 1867.

The war was over, and the slaves were free. Yet the sisters and
Weld knew that the former slaves needed both monetary and
educational assistance to enable them to rise economically and
socially. Many abolitionists went South after the war to establish schools for ex-slaves. Although Angelina and Sarah, at ages
sixty and seventy-two, were not strong enough to do this, they

did collect money and clothing for the freed slaves and worked for legislation to ensure their rights.

One day in February 1868, Angelina was at home reading the *National Anti-Slavery Standard*, the newspaper of the American Anti-Slavery Society, when she came across an article by a professor from Lincoln College, a school in Pennsylvania established for black students. The professor was arguing against the idea that blacks were intellectually inferior. As evidence he cited a brilliant student at Lincoln, a young man "by the name of Grimkie, who came here two years ago, just out of slavery."

Angelina's heart must have stopped for a moment as she read those words. *Grimkie. He must mean Grimké. Was he the son of a family slave? For the name Grimké was certainly uncommon.* Angelina showed the article to Theodore and Sarah. She wrote the young man a letter, identifying herself and asking him about himself.

Within days Archibald Grimké replied to Angelina's letter. Yes, he had heard about her and her sister, both through knowledge of the antislavery cause and through family members. *Indeed, his father was Henry Grimké, Angelina's brother, so that made him her nephew.* Again Angelina's heart must have stopped—a nephew she had never heard of! Over the next few months, letters between Archie and Angelina revealed the story of these other Grimkés' lives.

Henry had had three legitimate children with his wife Selina. He lived on his plantation, Cane Acre, with his family and about thirty slaves. Among them was the children's nurse, a strong, intelligent slave woman named Nancy Weston. After Selina died in the mid-1840s, Henry began living with Nancy. There is evidence of deep affection between them. With Nancy he had three sons—Archibald (Archie), Francis (Frank), and

John—but of course they were slaves and never were formally acknowledged as Henry's sons.

This situation, gruesome and horrifying to us today, was all too common in the South when slavery prevailed. Civil War diarist Mary Chesnut supplied penetrating comments on such peculiar familial relationships when she wrote in 1861:

> I wonder if it be a sin to think slavery a curse to any land. . . . God forgive us, but ours is a *monstrous* system and wrong and iniquity. . . . Like the patriarchs of old our men live all in one house with their wives and their concubines, and the mulattoes one sees in every family exactly resemble the white children—and every lady tells you who is the father of all the mulatto children in everybody's household, but those in her own she seems to think drop from the clouds, or pretends so to think.

In Henry's case, the two families were not living in the same house, since Selina had died and Henry's and her children were in boarding school or living on their own. Yet for his children with Nancy Weston it was all too true: they were their father's slaves.

In 1852 Henry had come down with typhoid fever when an epidemic swept the lowcountry of South Carolina. Nancy nursed him tirelessly, but he died within weeks. He had promised Nancy that although he could not free her (it was illegal to free slaves at that time in South Carolina), he would leave her and her children in the care of his eldest son, Montague, in whom, he told her, he had the "greatest confidence"; Archie told this to Angelina in a letter. Within months of Henry's death, Cane Acre Plantation, its slaves, its livestock—all were sold, except Nancy and her sons.

Angelina's sister Eliza, who was the executrix of Henry's will, brought Nancy and her family to Charleston, where they lived in poverty among the free black population. And if the Grimkés never helped them, neither did they disturb them. That is, until 1860, when Montague remarried and his second wife needed house slaves.

Archie, then twelve years old, was summoned to the Grimké household, where Montague—his white half-brother—and his wife lived with Eliza and Mary. Over Nancy's strong protests (what else could she do?), Archie became a house servant, although he was permitted to attend school and go home at night. Soon Frank was forced into service too.

Neither boy took well to the life of a house slave. Although both were very bright, they pretended to be stupid and rarely performed their duties as ordered. For example, Archie usually set the table incorrectly, causing Eliza to have to reset it after him. For major offenses, both boys were sent to the workhouse, where Charleston slaveowners sent slaves for severe punishments that they did not want to administer in person. Both boys were whipped there, although they were only thirteen and eleven years old.

Archie decided to run away. Helped by his mother, he was eventually hidden in a house in Charleston for over two years, until Charleston "fell" to the Union Army in February 1865. Frank also escaped Montague's grasp, running away to serve as a valet to a Confederate officer until he was caught and returned to Montague. This time Montague sold him, again to a Confederate officer. John was also enslaved by Montague and his family for a period of time.

At the war's end, Frank returned to Nancy's house and Archie came out of hiding. Although they lived in the same city, the two Grimké families had no contact with each other. Nancy's sons began to attend a new public school in Charleston, run by an abolitionist woman from Massachusetts

Francis, Archibald, and John Grimké,
Angelina's nephews, probably in the 1870s. Their mother, former
slave Nancy Weston, lived with Francis in his Washington, D.C.,
home until her death in 1895. *Courtesy of the Grimké Papers,*
*Moorland-Spingarn Research Center, Howard University*

named Frances Pillsbury. Mrs. Pillsbury was so struck with
Archie's and Frank's intelligence that she asked Nancy to permit them to further their education up North. Both Nancy and
her sons eagerly agreed. Eventually Archie and Frank came to
Lincoln College, where Angelina found them.

Angelina and Sarah were deeply moved by Archie's
story, and deeply ashamed of their family's behavior toward
these sons of Henry. Eliza—who had *lived* with them after

the war—*had never uttered a word about their existence.*
What could Angelina and Sarah do? For the sake of the
Grimké family name, for the sake of humanity, they had to
confront the past and try to rectify the sins of their family
against these young souls. As Angelina's daughter Sarah
later wrote, "Her brother had wronged these children; his
sisters must right them." They began by meeting the boys.
With her son Stuart, then twenty-nine years old, Angelina
traveled to Lincoln College in June 1868, to attend Archie's
and Frank's commencement. She stayed there a week, getting to know the two, discussing family history and the
young men's goals. Although Archie and Frank were glad to
meet this legend of abolitionism, they expected very little
from the relationship, undoubtedly based on their past history with the family.

In this they were surprised. They were embraced as long-
lost nephews by Angelina, Sarah, and Theodore. From then on,
they made regular visits to the Weld home in Hyde Park. Sarah
and Angelina advised them on graduate school, and if Archie
and Frank chose not to follow such advice, that was all right;
they were still beloved nephews. The Welds and Sarah contributed regularly their nephews' expenses, even when it
meant denying themselves. They sent money to Nancy in
Charleston, for John to come up North to study. John was not
the same caliber student as his brothers, however, and chose to
return to Charleston.

Eventually Archie enrolled in Harvard Law School and was
one of the first blacks to earn his law degree there. He became
a noted civil rights lawyer and early leader in the National
Association for the Advancement of Colored People (NAACP).
His only daughter, Angelina Weld Grimké, was born the year
after Angelina's death; this Angelina would later become a

well-known poet in the Harlem Renaissance of the 1920s. Frank graduated from Princeton Theological Seminary and for nearly fifty years served as pastor of the 15th Street Presbyterian Church in Washington, D.C. He married Charlotte Forten, whose parents had been Quaker friends of Sarah and Angelina in Philadelphia many decades earlier. Nancy Weston lived in Frank's house in Washington until her death in 1895.

Angelina and Theodore's own children had grown up and begun their own lives too. Stuart became a teacher and writer. He married and had one son, Lewis. Thody, of course, was incapacitated and never had a profession; yet he outlived both his parents and his older brother. Sarah married William Hamilton, a Unitarian minister in Hyde Park. They had four children, two of whom died in infancy. Eventually the Hamilton family moved to Michigan. Their daughter Angelina grew up to be a doctor, which undoubtedly would have gladdened her grandparents and great-aunt, had they lived to see it.

The woman's rights movement split in 1869. Differences of opinion between factions arose when the Fourteenth and Fifteenth Amendments to the Constitution were passed, guaranteeing the civil rights of all men, but not women. Some women believed that now was the time for women to get suffrage, others that this was the black man's hour and that women should do nothing to jeopardize it. The split also reflected contrasting ideas of how to achieve the goal of woman suffrage. The National Woman Suffrage Association, led by Elizabeth Cady Stanton and Susan B. Anthony, was the more radical group, focusing on a federal amendment but also on a variety of other concerns for women, such as legal, health, and educational issues. The American Woman Suffrage Association, led by Lucy Stone, held that all issues other than suffrage were irrelevant. This group concentrated its efforts on getting the franchise within individual states.

In 1870 Angelina and Sarah again made newspaper headlines for the cause of woman's rights. In February of that year, Angelina's friend Lucy Stone came to Hyde Park to lecture about a woman's right to vote. Led by sixty-five-year-old Angelina and seventy-seven-year-old Sarah, the women of Hyde Park determined to vote in the town election that was scheduled for the following month—even though it was not legal for women to vote in Massachusetts. They posted notices around town, informing people of a caucus, a meeting to recommend a slate of candidates. This meeting was held on March 4. They notified the election board of their intention to vote, and prepared themselves for this momentous step.

A furious snowstorm greeted the intrepid women on March 7, the day of the election. Nevertheless, they gathered in the local hotel lobby, where each lady was presented with a bouquet of flowers. Then, led by Angelina, Sarah, and Theodore, they marched down the street to the voting place. Many Hyde Park residents were outraged by this action; some found it ridiculous instead. The *New York Tribune* reported that "much opposition was manifested by the citizens, and when the women appeared . . . they were greeted by a storm of hisses and groans. . . ." Undeterred, the women deposited their ballots in a designated box, in protest "against [the] political ostracism of women." Of course, these ballots were not counted, *but this demonstration marked the first time any woman in the state of Massachusetts went to the polls.*

Sixty-five-year-old Angelina, and Sarah at seventy-two, cast ballots in their local Massachusetts town election, even though women did not have the right to vote in 1870. It would be fifty years before the Nineteenth Amendment to the Constitution, granting women the right to vote, would be passed. *Courtesy of the Hyde Park Historical Society, Boston, Massachusetts*

On December 23, 1873, Sarah Moore Grimké died at the age of eighty-one. On her death certificate in the space following "occupation," Theodore wrote, "Doing good." Angelina wrote to a friend, "You know what I have lost, not *a sister only*, but a mother, friend, counsellor,—everything I could lose in a woman."

The summer after Sarah's death, Angelina suffered a paralyzing stroke, and for the last five years of her life, her movements were severely restricted. Yet in her view of death, "all was light and peace"; she was not afraid. This light and peace came for Angelina on October 26, 1879. She was seventy-four years old.

She was buried near Sarah in an unmarked grave in the Weld family plot, on Evergreen Walk in Mount Hope Cemetery in Boston. At first it seems astounding that such an important historical figure would be lying in an unmarked grave. But upon reflection, one realizes that this is probably how the humble Angelina preferred it. Theodore joined the sisters in death in 1895, at the age of ninety-two.

Many veterans of the abolition and reform movements attended the memorial service for Angelina. Noted speakers were Lucy Stone, and Elizur Wright and Wendell Phillips of the American Anti-Slavery Society. William Lloyd Garrison had died in May of that year, and many other abolitionists were already dead.

Lucy Stone gave Angelina credit for the enormous impact she had on both the abolition and the woman's rights movements. She recalled:

> To those around her, [Angelina] seemed a quiet, gentle woman, devoted to her home, her husband, and her children. And such she was. But those whose memory

Theodore Weld,
as an older gentleman, was affectionately called "Father Weld" by many in his town. For many years he served as chairman of the committee which worked to establish a library in Hyde Park. Today the lecture hall there is named Weld Hall in his honor. *Courtesy of the Boston Athenaeum*

Angelina Grimké Weld,
the month before her death in 1879. Her stern countenance speaks eloquently of a life that, in Lucy Stone's words, "endured all the persecution which sectarian bigotry and proslavery hatred could devise." Photo by W.H. Barritt. *Courtesy of the Sophia Smith Collection, Smith College*

goes back to the time of fiery trials, in the early anti-slavery days, know that the world never held a nobler woman. The slaves' cause was her cause. She had counted the cost, renouncing everything. For their sake, she endured all the persecution which sectarian bigotry and proslavery hatred could devise against the first woman who dared to "speak in the church," or anywhere else in public, even for the slaves. It is impossible for those who today see and hear women as ministers and lecturers to understand the state of mind and feeling forty-three years ago, when no woman's voice was heard in public, and when the injunction for her to "keep silence" in the church was held to be as sacred as the commandment, "Thou shalt not steal". . . . The women of today owe more than they will ever know to the high courage, the rare insight, and fidelity to principle of this woman, by whose suffering easy paths have been made for them.

Wendell Phillips remembered her effect on the abolition movement of the 1830s:

When our cities roared with riot, when William Lloyd Garrison was dragged through the streets, when Dresser was mobbed in Nashville. . . . [N]o man who remembers 1837 and its lowering clouds will deny that there was hardly any contribution to the anti-slavery movement greater or more impressive than the crusade of these Grimké sisters from South Carolina through the New England States. . . . Were I to single out the moral and intellectual trait [in Angelina] which most won me, it was her serene indifference to the judgment of those about her. Self-poised, she seemed morally sufficient to herself.

Angelina Grimké paved the way for the next generation of women reformers to speak—the Abby Kelleys, the Lucy Stones, the Elizabeth Cady Stantons. Angelina was instrumental in pointing out prejudice in all places—North and South—a problem America has yet to solve. Her integrity, courage, and intense desire to better the world provide a model that supercedes the centuries. As Angelina herself once wrote, "I recognize no right but human rights."

# Appendix

## Angelina Grimké Weld's Speech in Pennsylvania Hall
## May 16, 1838

Men, brethren and fathers—mothers, daughters and sisters, what came ye out for to see? A reed shaken with the wind? Is it curiosity merely, or a deep sympathy with the perishing slave, that has brought this large audience together? [A yell from the mob without the building.]* Those voices without ought to awaken and call out our warmest sympathies. Deluded beings! "they know not what they do." They know not that they are undermining their own rights and their own happiness, temporal and eternal. Do you ask, "what has the North to do with slavery?" Hear it—hear it. Those voices without tell us that the very spirit of slavery is *here,* and has been roused to wrath by our abolition speeches and conventions: for surely liberty would not foam and tear herself with rage, because her friends are multiplied daily, and meetings are held in quick succession to set forth her virtues and extend her peaceful kingdom. This opposition shows that slavery has done its deadliest work in the hearts of our citizens. Do you ask, then, "what has the North to do?" I answer, cast out first the spirit of slavery from your own hearts, and then lend your aid to convert the South. Each one present has a work to do, be his or her situation what it may, however limited their means, or insignificant their supposed influence. The great men of this country will not do this work; the church will never do it.

---

*The bracketed remarks are by Samuel Webb, who was the treasurer of the Board of Managers of Pennsylvania Hall.

A desire to please the world, to keep the favor of all parties and of all conditions, makes them dumb on this and every other unpopular subject. They have become worldly-wise, and therefore God, in his wisdom, employs them not to carry on his plans of reformation and salvation. He hath chosen the foolish things of the world to confound the wise, and the weak to overcome the mighty.

As a Southerner I feel that it is my duty to stand up here tonight and bear testimony against slavery. I have seen it—I have seen it. I know it has horrors that can never be described. I was brought up under its wing: I witnessed for many years its demoralizing influences, and its destructiveness to human happiness. It is admitted by some that the slave is not happy under the *worst* forms of slavery. But I have *never* seen a happy slave. I have seen him dance in his chains, it is true; but he was not happy. There is a wide difference between happiness and mirth. Man cannot enjoy the former while his manhood is destroyed, and that part of the being which is necessary to the making, and to the enjoyment of happiness, is completely blotted out. The slaves, however, may be, and sometimes are, mirthful. When hope is extinguished, they say, "let us eat and drink, for to-morrow we die." [Just then stones were thrown at the windows,—a great noise without, and commotion within.] What is a mob? What would be the breaking of every window be? What would the leveling of this Hall be? Any evidence that we are wrong, or that slavery is a good and wholesome institution? What if the mob should now burst in upon us, break up our meeting and commit violence upon our persons—would this be anything compared with what the slaves endure? No, no: and we do not remember them "as bound with them," if we shrink in the time of peril, or feel unwilling to sacrifice ourselves, if need be, for their sake. [Great Noise.] I thank the Lord that there is yet left life enough to feel the truth, even though it rages at it—that conscience is not so completely seared as to be un-moved by the truth of the living God.

Many persons go to the South for a season, and are hos-pitably entertained in the parlor and at the table of the slave-holder. They never enter the huts of the slaves; they know nothing of the dark side of the picture, and they return home with praises on their lips of the generous character of those with whom they had tarried. Or if they have witnessed the cruelties of slavery, by remaining silent spectators they have naturally become callous—an insensibility has ensued which prepares them to apologize even for barbarity. Nothing but the corrupting influence of slavery on the hearts of the Northern people can induce them to apologize for it; and much will have been done for the destruction of Southern slavery when we have so reformed the North that no one here will be willing to risk his reputation by advocating or even excusing the hold-ing of men as property. The South know it, and acknowledge that as fast as our principles prevail, the hold of the master must be relaxed. [Another outbreak of mobocratic spirit, and some confusion in the house.]

How wonderfully constituted is the human mind! How it resists, as long as it can, all efforts made to reclaim from er-ror! I feel that all this disturbance is but an evidence that our efforts are the best that could have been adopted, or else the friends of slavery, would not care for what we say and do. The South know what we do. I am thankful that they are reached by our efforts. Many times I have wept in the land of my birth over the system of slavery. I know of none who sympathized in my feelings—I was unaware that any efforts were made to deliver the oppressed—no voice in the wilder-ness was heard calling on the people to repent and do works meet for repentance—and my heart sickened within me. Oh, how I should have rejoiced to know that such efforts as these were being made. I only wonder that I had such feelings. I wonder when I reflect under what influence I was brought up, that my heart is not harder than the nether millstone. But in the midst of temptation I was preserved, and my sympathy grew warmer, and my hatred of slavery more inveterate, until at last I have exiled myself from my native land because I could no longer endure to hear the wailing of the slave. I fled to the land of Penn; for here, thought I, sympathy for the slave will surely be found. But I found it not. The people were kind and hospitable, but the slave had no place in their thoughts. Whenever questions were put to me as to his condition, I felt that they were dictated by an idle curiosity, rather than by that deep feeling which would lead to effort for his rescue. I therefore shut up my grief in my own heart. I remembered that I was a Carolinian, from a state which framed this iniquity by law. I knew that throughout her territory was continued suffering, on the one part, and continual brutality and sin on the other. Every Southern breeze wafted to me the discordant tones of weeping and wailing, shrieks and groans, mingled with prayers and blasphemous curses. I thought there was no hope, that the wicked would go on in his wickedness, until he had destroyed both himself and his country. My heart sunk within me at the abominations in the midst of which I had been born and educated. What will it avail, cried I in bitterness of spirit, to expose to the gaze of strangers the horrors and pollutions of slavery, when there is no ear to hear nor heart to feel and pray for the slave. The language of my soul was, "Oh tell it not in Gath, publish it not in the streets of Askelon." But how different do I feel now! Animated with hope, nay, with an assurance of the triumph of liberty and good will to man, I will lift up my voice like a trumpet, and show this people their transgression, their sins of omission towards the slave, and what they can do towards affecting Southern mind, and overthrowing Southern oppression.

We may talk of occupying neutral ground, but on this subject, in its present attitude, there is no such thing as neutral ground. He that is not for us is against us, and he that gathereth not with us, scattereth abroad. If you are on what you suppose to be neutral ground, the South look upon you as on the side of the oppressor. And is there one who loves his country willing to give his influence, even indirectly, in favor of slavery—that curse of nations? God swept Egypt with the besom of destruction, and punished Judea also with a sore punishment, because of slavery. And have we any reason to believe that he is less just now?—or that he will be more favorable to us than to his own "peculiar people?" [Shoutings, stones thrown against the windows, etc.]

There is nothing to be feared from those who would stop our mouths, but they themselves should fear and tremble. The current is even now setting fast against them. If the arm of the North had not caused the Bastille of slavery to totter to its foundation, you would not hear those cries. A few years ago, and the South felt secure, and with a contemptuous sneer asked, "Who are the abolitionists? The abolitionists are nothing?"—Ay, in one sense they were nothing, and they are nothing still. But in this we rejoice, that "God has chosen things that are not to bring to nought things that are." [Mob again disturbed the meeting.]

We often hear the question asked, "What shall we do?" Here is an opportunity for doing something now. Every man and every woman present may do something by showing that we fear not a mob, and, in the midst of threatenings and revilings, by opening our mouths for the dumb and pleading the cause of those who are ready to perish.

To work as we should in this cause, we must know what Slavery is. Let me urge you then to buy the books which have been written on this subject and read them, and then lend them to your neighbors. Give your money no longer for things which pander to pride and lust, but aid in scattering "the living coals of truth" upon the naked heart of this nation,—in circulating appeals to the sympathies of Christians in behalf of the outraged and suffering slave. But, it is said by some, our "books and papers do not speak the truth." Why, then, do they not contradict what we say? They cannot. Moreover the South has entreated, nay commanded us to be silent; and what greater evidence of the truth of our publications could be desired?

Women of Philadelphia! allow me as a Southern woman, with much attachment to the land of my birth, to entreat you to come up to this work. Especially let me urge you to petition. Do you say, "It does no good?" The South already turns pale at the number sent. They have read the reports of the proceedings of Congress, and there have seen that among other petitions were very many from the women of the North on the subject of slavery. This fact has called the attention of the South to the subject. How could we expect to have done more as yet? Men who hold the rod over slaves, rule in the councils of the nation: and they deny our right to petition and to remonstrate against abuses of our sex and of our kind. We have these rights, however, from our God. Only let us exercise them: and though often turned away unanswered, let us remember the influence of importunity upon the unjust judge, and act accordingly. The fact that the South look with jealousy upon our measures shows that they are effectual. There is, therefore, no cause for doubting or despair, but rather for rejoicing.

It was remarked in England that women did much to abolish Slavery in her colonies. Nor are they now idle. Numerous petitions from them have recently been presented to the Queen, to abolish the apprenticeship with its cruelties nearly equal to those of the system whose place it supplies. One petition two miles and a quarter long has been presented. And do you think these labors will be in vain? Let the history of the past answer. When the women of these States send up to Congress such a petition, our legislators will arise as did those of England, and say, "When all the maids and matrons of the land are knocking at our doors we must legislate." Let the zeal and love, the faith and works of our English sisters quicken ours—that while the slaves continue to suffer, and when they shout deliverance, we may feel the satisfaction of *having done what we could.*

From *History of Pennsylvania Hall, Which Was Destroyed by a Mob, on the 17th of May, 1838,* edited by Samuel Webb (Philadelphia: Merrihew and Gunn, 1838). Reprinted in *History of Woman Suffrage,* Vol. I, by Elizabeth C. Stanton, Susan B. Anthony, and Matilda J. Gage (New York: Fowler and Wells, 1881-1922).

LETTER FROM EX-SLAVE HESTER SNOWDEN TO ANGELINA GRIMKÉ*

Charleston, May 6, 1831

Dear Miss Angelina,

I address you humbly as a Christian Friend and hope that you will [be] gratified to read a few lines expressive of affectionate regard from one who sincerely feels it. I have received your kind message through Maria. I think I can say with some confidence I am not weary of well doing, but am striving to run with patience the race set before me [?]. I delight in prayer, and often remember your grace [?] when on my knees. I enjoy much happiness in being a disciple of Christ. I adore the mercy that has brought me to know and feel my need of him. There

---

[*It is likely that this letter was dictated to a white person, who modified the language to conform to the letter-writing conventions of the time.]

has been a great revival in our Church. Many have found peace to their souls in believing. Oh when will the blessed period arrive when all nations shall flock to Christ as doves to the windows takeing no rest until they find him. I know not how to express my gratitude to you, who was the instrument of leading me to the hope I now possess. You first taught me to know I was a sinner—and may you experience the blessed reward—promised to those who convert a soul from the error of their ways. Will you be so kind as to write me an answer to this and when go to the throne of peace remember poor Hester. And if we no more are permitted to meet here may we spend an eternity of bliss together where all distinctions of Christian people and tongues are lost in the glory of our Redeemer.

Affectionately and respectfully,
your humble friend,
Hester Snowden

P.S. Stephen Grimké [a slave belonging to the Grimké family; this may be the same Stephen referred to in chapter 9] desires me to tell you he is very grateful to you for your letter. It has had a happy effect on him. He feels a renewed earnestness in endeavouring [to] be entirely conformed to the will of God in Jesus Christ.

*[in Angelina's handwriting]*
The writer of the above was personally known to me in Charleston. When first awakened to the sense of my own sinfulness and the importance of the salvation of the soul one of my first concerns was to teach the poor ignorant slaves. Besides having family prayers morning and evening, I also called our servants to gather twice every week after tea, and read and explained the Scriptures to them. At these little meet-

ings the neighbors' servants often attended, and Hester was one of these. She often appeared completely broken up under the instructions given forth and that which was sown [?] in weakness seemed [?] to be raised in power.

Weld-Grimké Papers, Clements Library, University of Michigan

LETTER FROM ANGELINA GRIMKÉ TO WILLIAM LLOYD GARRISON
AUGUST 30, 1835

Respected Friend:

It seems as if I was compelled at this time to address thee, notwithstanding all my reasoning against intruding on thy valuable time, and the uselessness of so insignificant a person as myself offering thee the sentiments of sympathy at this alarming crisis.

I can hardly express to thee the deep and solemn interest with which I have viewed the violent proceedings of the last few weeks. Although I expected opposition, yet I was not pre-pared for it so soon—it took me by surprise, and I greatly feared Abolitionists would be driven back in the first onset, and thrown into confusion. So fearful was I, that though I clung with unflinching firmness to our principles, yet I was afraid of even opening one of thy papers, lest I should see some indication of compromise, some surrender, some palliation. Under these feelings, I was urged to read thy Appeal to the cit-izens of Boston. Judge, then, what were my feelings on finding that my fears were utterly groundless, and that thou stoodest firm in the midst of the storm, determined to suffer and to die, rather than yield one inch. My heart was filled with thanksgiving and praise to the Preserver of men; I thanked God, and took courage, earnestly desiring that thousands may adopt thy language, and be prepared to meet the Martyr's doom, rather than give up the principles you (i.e. Abolitionists) have adopted. The ground upon which you stand is holy ground: never—never surrender it. If you surrender it, the hope of the slave is extinguished, and the chains of his servitude will be strengthened a hundred fold. But let no man take your crown, and success is as certain as the rising of tomorrow's sun. But remember you must be willing to suffer the loss of all things— willing to be the scorn and reproach of professor and profane. You must obey our great Master's injunction: "Fear not them that kill the body, and after that, have nothing more that they can do." You must, like Apostles, "count not your lives dear unto yourselves, so that you may finish your course with joy."

Religious persecution always begins with mobs: it is always unprecedented in the age or country in which it commences, and therefore there are no laws, by which Reformers can be punished; consequently, a lawless band of unprincipled men determined to take the matter into their hands, and act out in mobs, what they know are the principles of a large majority of those who are too high in Church and State to condescend to mingle with them, though they secretly approve and rejoice over their violent measures. The first martyr who ever died, was stoned by a lawless mob; and if we look at the rise of various sects—Methodists, Friends, &c.—we shall find that mobs began the persecution against them, and that it was not until after the people had thus spoken out their wishes, that laws were framed to fine, imprison, or destroy them. Let us, then, be prepared for the enactment of laws even in our Free States, against Abolitionists. And how ardently has the prayer been breathed, that God would prepare us for all he is preparing for us; that he would strengthen us in the hour of conflict, and cover our heads (if consistent with his holy will) in the day of battle! But O! how earnestly have I desired, not that we may escape suffering, but that we may be willing to endure unto the end. If we call upon the slave-holder to suffer the loss of what he calls property, then let us show him we make this demand from a deep sense of duty, by being ourselves willing to suffer the loss of character, property—yes, and life itself, in what we believe to be the cause of bleeding humanity.

My mind has been especially turned toward those, who are standing in the fore front of the battle; and the prayer has gone up for their preservation—not the preservation of their lives, but the preservation of their minds in humility and patience, faith, hope, and charity—that charity which is the bond of perfectness. If persecution is the means which God has ordained for the accomplishment of this great end, EMANCIPATION; then, in dependence upon Him for strength to bear it, I feel as if I could say, LET IT COME; for it is my deep, solemn, deliberate conviction, that this is a cause worth dying for. I say so, from what I have seen, and heard, and known, in a land of slavery, where rests the darkness of Egypt, and where is found the sin of Sodom. Yes! LET IT COME—let us suffer, rather than insurrections should arise.

At one time, I thought this system would be overthrown in blood, with the confused noise of the warrior; but a hope gleams across my mind, that our blood will be spilt, instead of the slave-holders'; our lives will be taken, and theirs spared— I say a hope, for all things I desire to be spared the anguish of seeing our beloved country desolated with the horrors of a servile war. If persecution can abolish slavery, it will also purify the Church; and who that stands between the porch and altar, weeping over the sins of the people, will not be willing to suffer, if such immense good will be accomplished. Let us endeavor, then, to put on the whole armor of God, and, having done all, to stand ready for whatever is before us.

I have just heard of Dresser's being flogged: it is no surprise at all; but the language of our Lord has been sweetly revived—

"Blessed are ye when men shall revile you, and persecute you, and say all manner of evil against you falsely, for my sake. Rejoice, and be exceedingly glad, for great is your reward in heaven." O! for a willingness and strength to suffer! But we shall have false brethren now, just as the Apostles had, and this will be one of our greatest griefs.

A. E. Grimké

Printed in *The Liberator*, September 19, 1835.

## ANGELINA GRIMKÉ'S SPEECH BEFORE THE LEGISLATIVE COMMITTEE OF THE MASSACHUSETTS STATE LEGISLATURE, FEBRUARY 21, 1838

Mr. Chairman—

More than 2000 years have rolled their dark and bloody waters down the rocky, winding channel of Time into the broad ocean of Eternity, since woman's voice was heard in the palace of an eastern monarch, and woman's petition achieved the salvation of millions of her race from the edge of the sword. The Queen of Persia [the Hebrew Queen Esther],—if Queen she might be called, who was but the mistress of her voluptuous lord,— trained as she had been in the secret abominations of an oriental harem, had studied too deeply the character of Ahasuerus not to know that the sympathies of his heart could not be reached, except through the medium of his sensual appetites. Hence we find her arrayed in royal apparel, and standing in the inner court of the King's house, hoping by her personal charms to win the favor of her lord. And after the golden sceptre had been held out, and the inquiry was made, "What wilt thou, Queen Esther, and what is thy request? it shall be given thee to the half of the kingdom"—even then she dared not ask either for her own life, or that of her people. She felt that if her mission of mercy was to be successful, his animal propensities must be still more powerfully wrought upon—the luxurious feast must be prepared, the banquet of wine must be served up, and the favorable moment must be seized when, gorged with gluttony and intoxication, the king's heart was fit to be operated upon by the pathetic appeal, "If I have found favor in thy sight, O King, and if it please the King, let my life be given at my petition; and my people at my request." It was thus, through personal charms, and sensual gratification, and individual influence, that the Queen of Persia obtained the precious boon she craved,—her own life, and the life of her beloved people.

Mr. Chairman, it is my privilege to stand before you on a similar mission of life and love; but I thank God that we live in an age of the world too enlightened and too moral to admit of the adoption of the same means to obtain as holy an end. I feel that it would be an insult to this Committee, were I to attempt to win their favor by arraying my person in gold, and silver, and costly apparel, or by inviting them to partake of the luxurious feast, or the banquet of wine. I understand the spirit of the age too well to believe that you could be moved by such sensual means—means as unworthy of you, as they would be beneath the dignity of the cause of humanity. Yes, I feel that if you are reached at all, it will not be by me, but by the truths I shall endeavor to present to your understandings and your hearts. The heart of the eastern despot was reached through the lowest propensities of his animal nature, by personal influence; yours, I know, cannot be reached but through the loftier sentiments of the intellectual and moral feelings.

Let the history of the world answer these queries. Read the denunciations of Jehovah against the follies and crimes of Israel's daughters. Trace the influence of woman as a courtezan and a mistress in the destinies of nations, both ancient and modern, and see her wielding her power too often to debase and destroy, rather than to elevate and save. It is often said that women rule the world, through their influence over men. If so, then may we well hide our faces in the dust, and cover ourselves with sackcloth and ashes. It has not been by moral power and intellectual, but through the baser passions of man. This dominion of women must be resigned—the sooner the better; "in the age which is approaching, she should be something more—she should be a citizen; and this title, which demands an increase of knowledge and of reflection, opens before her a new empire."

I stand before you as a southerner, exiled from the land of my birth, by the sound of the lash, and the piteous cry of the slave. I stand before you as a repentant slaveholder. I stand before you as a moral being, endowed with precious and inalienable rights, which are correlative with solemn duties and high responsibilities; and as a moral being I feel that I owe it to the suffering slave, and to the deluded master, to my country and the world, to do all that I can to overturn a system of complicated crimes, built up upon the broken hearts and prostrate bodies of my countrymen in chains, and cemented by the blood and sweat and tears of my sisters in bonds.

[The remainder of Angelina's speech focused on the merits of the petitions she presented.]

Printed in *The Liberator*, March 2, 1838.

# TIME LINE OF
# ANGELINA GRIMKÉ'S LIFE IN AMERICAN HISTORY

|  |  |  |
|---|---|---|
|  | 1776 | Declaration of Independence |
|  | 1789 | French Revolution begins |
| Sarah Moore Grimké born; November 26 | 1792 |  |
| Theodore Dwight Weld born; November 23 | 1803 | Louisiana Purchase |
| Angelina Emily Grimké born; February 20 | 1805 |  |
|  | 1808 | Foreign slave trade ended |
| Angelina refuses confirmation | 1818 |  |
| Judge Grimké dies | 1819 |  |
|  | 1820 | Missouri Compromise |
| Sarah moves to Philadelphia | 1821 |  |
| Angelina converts to Presbyterianism | 1826 |  |
| Angelina moves to Philadelphia | 1829 |  |
|  | 1831 | *The Liberator* published; Nat Turner Revolt |
|  | 1832 | Nullification Crisis |
| Thomas Smith Grimké dies; Theodore Weld withdraws from Lane Seminary | 1834 |  |

| | | |
|---|---|---|
| Angelina writes to William Lloyd Garrison | 1835 | |
| Angelina writes *Appeal to the Christian Women of the South*; Angelina begins speaking in New York | 1836 | Texas declares independence |
| Grimké sisters speak in Massachusetts | 1837 | Panic of 1837 |
| Angelina marries Theodore Weld | 1838 | |
| *American Slavery as It Is* published; Charles Stuart Faucheraud Weld born | 1839 | |
| Welds move to Belleville, New Jersey | 1840 | World Anti-Slavery Convention in London |
| Theodore Grimké Weld born | 1841 | |
| Sarah Grimké Weld born | 1844 | |
| | 1846 | Mexican War begins |
| | 1848 | Woman's Rights Convention in Seneca Falls |
| | 1850 | Compromise of 1850 |
| | 1852 | *Uncle Tom's Cabin* published |
| Welds start Eagleswood School | 1854 | Kansas-Nebraska Act passed |
| | 1859 | John Brown raids Harpers Ferry |
| | 1860 | Abraham Lincoln elected president |
| | 1861 | Civil War begins |

| | | |
|---|---|---|
| Welds move to Massachusetts | 1863 | |
| | 1865 | Civil War ends; slavery abolished |
| | 1869 | Transcontinental railroad; Fifteenth Amendment passed; woman's suffrage movement splits |
| Sarah and Angelina "vote" | 1870 | |
| Sarah dies; December 23 | 1873 | |
| Angelina dies; October 26 | 1879 | Thomas Edison invents incandescent lamp |
| | 1884 | Eleanor Roosevelt born |
| | 1889 | Jane Addams opens Hull House |
| | 1890 | National American Woman's Suffrage Association |
| Theodore Weld dies; February 3 | 1895 | |
| | 1901 | Theodore Roosevelt assumes presidency |

# SELECTED BIBLIOGRAPHY

## PUBLISHED WORKS

Abzug, Robert H. *Passionate Liberator: Theodore Dwight Weld and the Dilemma of Reform*. New York: Oxford University Press, 1980.

Bacon, Margaret H. *The Quiet Rebels: The Story of the Quakers in America*. New York: Basic Books, 1969.

———. *Valiant Friend: The Life of Lucretia Mott*. New York: Walker and Co., 1980.

Birney, Catherine H. *The Grimké Sisters: Sarah and Angelina Grimké: The First Women Advocates of Abolition and Woman's Rights*. Boston: Lee and Shepard, 1885; reprinted 1970 by Scholarly Press, St. Clair Shores, Michigan.

Blackwell, Alice Stone. *Lucy Stone: Pioneer of Woman's Rights*. Boston: Little, Brown, 1930.

Bruce, Dickson D., Jr. *Archibald Grimké: Portrait of a Black Independent*. Baton Rouge: Louisiana State University Press, 1993.

Ceplair, Larry, ed. *The Public Years of Sarah and Angelina Grimké: Selected Writings, 1835–1839*. New York: Columbia University Press, 1989.

Chesnut, Mary Boykin Miller. *Mary Chesnut's Civil War*. Edited by C. Vann Woodward. New Haven, CT: Yale University Press, 1981.

Dumond, Dwight L. *Antislavery Origins of the Civil War in the United States*. Ann Arbor: University of Michigan Press, 1959.

————. *Antislavery: The Crusade for Freedom in America*. Ann Arbor: University of Michigan Press, 1961.

Filler, Louis. *The Crusade Against Slavery, 1830–1860*. New York: Harper, 1960.

Flexner, Eleanor. *Century of Struggle: The Woman's Rights Movement in the United States*. Cambridge, MA: Harvard University Press, 1975.

Fraser, Walter F., Jr. *Charleston! Charleston! The History of a Southern City*. Columbia: University of South Carolina Press, 1989.

Grimké, Angelina Emily. *Appeal to the Christian Women of the South*. New York: American Anti-Slavery Society, 1836.

————. *An Appeal to the Women of the Nominally Free States; Issued by an Anti-Slavery Convention of the American Women & Held by Adjournment from the 9th to the 12th of May, 1837*. 1st ed. New York: W. S. Dorr, 1837.

Koch, Adrienne. "A Family Crisis: Letters from John Faucheraud Grimké and Thomas Smith Grimké to Henry Grimké, 1818," *The South Carolina Historical Magazine*, Vol. 69, No. 3, July 1968, pp. 171–92.

————. "Two Charlestonians in Pursuit of Truth," *The South Carolina Historical Magazine*, Vol. 69, No. 3, July 1968, pp. 159–170.

Lerner, Gerda. *The Grimké Sisters from South Carolina*. New York: Schocken, 1967.

*The Liberator*, Vol. V, No. 45, November 7, 1835.

————. Vol. VIII, No. 21, May 25, 1838.

Lumpkin, Katharine DuPre. *The Emancipation of Angelina Grimké*. Chapel Hill: University of North Carolina Press, 1974.

Miller, Annie Elizabeth. *Our Family Circle*. Marietta, GA: Continental Book Co., 1957.

Peck, George T. *What Is Quakerism? A Primer*. Wallingford, PA: Pendle Hill Publications, 1988.

Sherwin, Oscar. *Prophet of Liberty: The Life and Times of Wendell Phillips*. New York: Bookman Associates, 1958.

Stanton, Elizabeth C. "Angelina Grimké: Reminiscences," in Stanton, Elizabeth C., Anthony, Susan B., and Gage, Matilda J. *History of Woman Suffrage*. 6 vols. New York: Fowler & Wells, 1881–1922. Vol. I, pp. 392–406.

Sterling, Dorothy. *Ahead of Her Time: Abby Kelley and the Politics of Antislavery*. New York: W. W. Norton, 1991.

Thomas, Benjamin P. *Theodore Weld: Crusader for Freedom*. New Brunswick, NJ: Rutgers University Press, 1950.

Wainwright, Nicholas, ed. *A Philadelphia Perspective: The Diary of Sidney George Fisher, Covering the Years 1834–1871*. Philadelphia: Historical Society of Pennsylvania, 1967.

Weld, Theodore Dwight. *In Memory, Angelina Grimké Weld*. Boston: G. H. Ellis, 1880.

[Weld, Theodore Dwight]. *American Slavery as it is: Testimony of a Thousand Witnesses*. New York: American Anti-Slavery Society, 1839.

————. Angelina Grimké Weld, and Sarah M. Grimké. *Letters of Theodore Dwight Weld, Angelina Grimké Weld and Sarah Grimké: 1822–1844*. Barnes, G. H., and Dumond, D. W., editors. 2 vols. New York: D. Appleton-Century Co., 1934.

## UNPUBLISHED WORKS

Grimké family papers, 1761–1866. South Carolina Historical Society Collections, Charleston, South Carolina.

Phone interview, Batson Hewitt, realtor, Charleston, South Carolina, 9/8/97.

Weld-Grimké papers, 1822–1898. William L. Clements Library, University of Michigan, Ann Arbor, Michigan.

# INDEX

27986

27986